Becoming Human

The Goshen Conference on Religion and Science

The Goshen Conference on Religion and Science, a yearly lecture series, features distinguished scholars. The proceedings are edited by Carl S. Helrich and published by Pandora Press.

Religion and Science: God, Evolution and the Soul
Nancy Murphy (2001)

A Universe of Ethics Morality and Hope
George F. R. Ellis (2002)

The Dialogue between Science and Religion
Antje Jackelén (2003)

Purpose, Evolution and the Mystery of Life
John F. Haught (2004)

Cosmology, Evolution, and Resurrection Hope
Robert John Russell (2005)

Religion-and-Science as Spiritual Quest for Meaning
Philip Hefner (2006)

The Evolution of Terrestrial and Extraterrestrial Life
Ted Peters (2007)

Science and Origins: Probing the Deeper Questions
Holmes Rolston III (2008)

The Limits of Perfection
Noreen Hertzfeld (2009)

Worrying About Evolution
Owen Gingerich (2011)

Re-Imaging the Divine Image
Celia Deane-Drummond (2012)

Becoming Human
Gayle Woloschak (2013)

Becoming Human

Weaving Together Genetics and Personhood

Proceedings of the Thirteenth Annual
Goshen Conference on Religion and Science

Gayle Woloschak

Professor of Radiation Oncology, Radiology,
and Cell and Molecular Biology
Northwestern University
Associate Director of the Zygon Center for Religion and Science
Adjunct Professor of Religion and Science
Lutheran School of Theology at Chicago

Edited by Carl S. Helrich
Goshen College

PANDORA
PRESS

Library and Archives Canada Cataloguing in Publication

Woloschak, Gayle E., author
        Becoming human : weaving together genetics and
personhood / Gayle Woloschak ; edited by Carl S. Helrich.

Includes index.
Based on papers presented at the Goshen Conference on Religion
        and Science, Goshen, Indiana, April 5-7.
ISBN 978-1-926599-59-5 (softcover)

        1. Human genetics--Religious aspects--Christianity--Congresses.
2. Human beings--Religious aspects--Christianity--Congresses.
I. Helrich, Carl S., editor II. Annual Goshen Conference on Religion
and Science (13th : 2013 : Goshen, Ind.) III. Title.

BL255.W65 2017   215'.7   C2017-906260-3

Published by Pandora Press

Cover woodcut by Tatjana Paunesku

ISBN 978-1-926599-59-5

Acknowledgements

The author would like to thank the audience and organizers of the Goshen Conference for their work in putting this volume together. The text of the questions and discussions are captured well here, but what is not so easily found in these pages is the enthusiasm and energy that is expressed by this group. The Goshen Conference is a shining light in the science-religion world!

Contents

Editor's Preface

In each annual Goshen Conference on Religion and Science a single speaker, who has proven to be an important voice in the dialogue between religion and science, is invited to present a topic of her or his choice in a series of three lectures. Most of the conference is then devoted to monitored discussions in which the participants engage the speaker's ideas. There is also a worship service with a homily presented by one of the participants in the conference.

The three lectures, the homily, and an edited version of the discussions are presented here. The reader will find many of the questions she or he may have, after reading the lectures, raised in these discussions.

The speaker for the 2013 conference was Gayle Woloschak, who is Professor of Radiation Oncology, Radiology, and Cell and Molecular Biology at the Feinberg School of Medicine, Northwestern University. She also holds a DMin degree from Pittsburgh Theological Seminary and is currently Associate Director of the Zygon Center for Religion and Science, director of the Epic of Creation program, and Adjunct Professor of Religion and Science at the Lutheran School of Theology at Chicago.

Simply stated, Gayle is an academic scientist with a deep interest in students and their education, who is a Christian religious scholar with a theology degree. She is also an active member of her church, which is Eastern Orthodox.

Gayle brought all of her background as well as her curiosity and willingness to probe even unfamiliar issues, to the conference. The reader will see this in the Discussions section of these proceedings. Gayle was able to make the theology alive and practical, as well as scholarly, in her responses to wide ranging questions and comments.

Some of the discussions were complex, and even difficult, because Gayle opened some boxes that are often not considered from a combination of both a religious and a scientific perspective. And the questions and comments raised are from participants without biblical or scientific references before them. In some of these instances I have attempted, as the editor, to provide the biblical references necessary to make the issues clear.

As an example, at one point the question of the thoughts and even emotions of God was encountered. When we try to consider thoughts and emotions of God we enter the deep unknown. But it does not help to simply close the door. At one point Gayle entered that arena with reference to the considerations of the Homilist, Peggy Schott, who is also a scientist at Northwestern.

Gayle used the masculine pronoun for God. I have made no attempt to edit that. Were the speaker a man I would have done so. But I have chosen to keep the pronoun she chose, leaving any discomfort as something with which the reader must deal.

Carl Helrich
Goshen College
June 2016

Lectures

The speaker presents the topic for the conference in three lectures. These are carefully prepared and may be considered authoritative statements of the speaker's position at the time of the conference.

1. Humans in Light of Genetics

Introduction

This series of lectures will deal with the topic of humanity and the human person. In the first two lectures we will discuss humans in the context of our genetics, epigenetics and environment. In the final lecture we will reflect theologically on the human person. In the beginning, I would like to make some comments about the broad science-religion dialogue to put some of this in context.

I heard a joke about the rabbi and the Pope that I think is relevant to this discussion:

> Several centuries ago, the Pope decreed that all the Jews had to convert to Catholicism or leave Italy. There was a huge outcry from the Jewish community, so the Pope offered a deal: he'd have a religious debate with the leader of the Jewish community. If the Jews won, they could stay in Italy; if the Pope won, they'd have to convert or leave. The Jewish people met and picked an aged and wise rabbi to represent them in the debate. However, as the rabbi spoke no Italian, and the Pope spoke no Yiddish, they agreed that it would be a 'silent' debate. On the chosen day the Pope and rabbi sat opposite each other. The Pope raised his hand and showed three fingers. The rabbi looked back and raised one finger. Next, the Pope waved his finger around his head. The rabbi pointed to the ground where he sat. The Pope brought out a

communion wafer and a chalice of wine. The rabbi pulled out an apple. With that, the Pope stood up and declared himself beaten and said that the rabbi was too clever. The Jews could stay in Italy.

Later the cardinals met with the Pope and asked him what had happened. The Pope said, 'First I held up three fingers to represent the Trinity. He responded by holding up a single finger to remind me there is still only one God common to both our beliefs. Then, I waved my finger around my head to show him that God was all around us. The rabbi responded by pointing to the ground to show that God was also right here with us. I pulled out the wine and wafer to show that God absolves us of all our sins, and the rabbi pulled out an apple to remind me of the original sin. He bested me at every move and I could not continue.'

Meanwhile, the Jewish community gathered to ask the rabbi how he'd won. 'I haven't a clue,' said the rabbi. 'First, he told me that we had three days to get out of Italy, so I gave him the finger. Then he tells me that the whole country would be cleared of Jews and I told him that we were staying right here.'

'And then what?' asked a woman. 'Who knows?' said the rabbi. 'He took out his lunch so I took out mine.'

This joke is about two people who are talking to each other but who are not communicating. Let us hope that they are not representative of the science-religion dialogue where people are talking at each other but not really able to connect.

A number of years ago a series of surveys were taken regarding scientists. When children were asked what they thought about scientists; they said scientists speak a foreign language that no one can understand, that they live underground, that they wear white coats even when they sleep, they wear glasses, and they don't require food. While some of these are true, they do reflect a lack of reality about scientists and how they function today. Nevertheless, perhaps the surveys done of adults asking them what they thought about scientists are even more interesting. Adults said, scientists speak a language that no one can understand, that they are antisocial, and that they have cured diseases but only rich people can get the cures. These comments by adults reflect not only a fear of scientists but also a distrust of them.

We must realize that scientists and science impact humanity in many different ways. Scientists help us to understand the world around us. The practice of medicine involves diagnosis and treatment of disease that touches all parts of our population. This practice involves quality of life concerns, beginning of life issues, end of life matters, and much more. Through ecology and environmental concerns, we have examined the importance of wetlands, rain forests, and other dwindling environmental niches. Concerns about genetically-modified (GMO) foods are found everywhere. Issues of technology include not only computers and iPads but also genetic diagnosis of disease, genetic counseling, and gene therapies. With each year the impact of science on society grows.

It is important to note that science frequently is a driver for ethical decisions. One of the best examples in modern times came with the discovery that HIV causes AIDS and the finding that HIV is transmitted through body fluids. In the early days when it was not known how the virus was spread, it was reasonable to consider quarantining and restricting access of those who were infected; in fact, there was even discussion about limiting aid to those who were infected. After science demonstrated the route of viral transmission, that is that it was spread through body fluids and not through airborne routes, then it became unreasonable to restrict any person with AIDS. Knowledge gained from science impacts the decisions so that they could be made ethically. To quarantine a person with HIV was no longer ethical. In fact, it became possible for people with HIV infections to live with uninfected people. The facts shaped the understanding of the disease, and therefore they shaped the ethical treatment of patients.[1]

I do not mean to say by this that science somehow has precedence over other forms of knowledge. As the great scholar Francisco Ayala wrote,

> … science is a way of knowing, but it is not the only way. Knowledge also derives from other sources, such as common sense, artistic and religious experience, and philosophical reflection.[2]

---

[1] Gayle E. Woloschak, "HIV: How science shaped the ethics," *Zygon* 38, no. 1 (2003): 163-167; Gayle E. Woloschak, "The New Biology and Its Impact in Biomedical Strategies Against HIV/AIDS," *Zygon* 39, no. 2 (2004): 477-486.

[2] Francisco Ayala, *Theology and Science* 2 (2003): 9-32.

1. Who are we?

The first question I would like to address is "who are we"; who are we as human beings, and what is the human person. In the context of our evolution, our genetics, and our culture, it becomes difficult to define the human person. Are we a population or are we individuals, persons? Are we mere animals or are we something different? How do we think? How do other animals think? When does human life begin? When does it end? The answers may not be only in the science but they are made more difficult by the science. There are discoveries that have made the question of "who are we?" more complicated in recent years. Evolution tells us that humans are animals; genetics shows that we share a genetic code with other species; comparative genetics demonstrates that we are 99% identical with chimps; embryology cannot decide when life begins; and in the cognitive sciences we see that science cannot decide when life ends.

While recent studies have shown that there is only a 1% difference in genetic sequence between chimps and humans, looking at the two species suggest that those differences are very important. While the majority of priteins made by the two species are identical, studies of how genes are turned on and turned off that have pointed to the major differences between chimps and humans. Gene expression patterns in the human brain have changed more dramatically during evolution than gene expression in the chimp brain. About 400 genes in the brain are more abundantly expressed in humans than in chimps. Similar changes in gene expression are not found in other organs, for example the liver. These results suggest that human brain differences are the result of accumulated mutations in regions of genes that regulate gene expression patterns and not in the portions that code for proteins.[3]

Recent studies have determined the complete sequences of over eighty different human genomes. These studies have shown a great diversity within the human population, much more diversity than is found among many other mammalian species. Comparisons among humans have shown not only small mutations, but also differences with large gene insertions, deletions, and inversions in hundreds of different loci.[4]

---

[3] Elizabeth Pennisi, "Mining the molecules that made our mind," *Science* 313 (2006): 1908-1911.
[4] Jeffrey M. Kidd, et al., "Mapping and sequencing of structural variation from eight human genomes," *Nature* 453 (2008): 56-64.

There have been several research groups that have explored the genomes of Neanderthals, a subspecies of modern humans *Homo sapiens*. Initial studies looked only at the sequences of mitochondria, small subcellular organelles that have their own DNA independent of nuclear DNA in cells. These studies demonstrated that Neaderthals had 5-20% DNA that overlaps with modern humans.[5] This suggests that interbreeding among Neaderthals and modern humans may have occurred at some time in the distant past. Comparisons of nuclear genetic sequences in humans and Neanderthals have revealed major differences in several areas.[6] Genes associated with Type II Diabetes were not found in Neanderthals suggesting that there were energy metabolism differences between Neanderthals and modern humans. Genes associated with cognitive disorders (autism, schizophrenia, others) are also not found in Neaderthals while they are found in modern humans. In general, it is possible that cognitive capabilities of modern human were also associated with the development of cognitive disorders; in fact, the development of cognitive disorders may be the price we modern humans pay for cognitive function we have today. Finally, genes associated with rib cage shape and shoulder joint structure, which form the basis for shape differences between Neanderthals and modern humans are also different, all indicative of structural changes associated with the development of modern humans.

Related to the issue of human development is the development and legacy of human culture. The concept "survival of the fittest" or natural selection is used in evolution to describe how there is a selection pressure to retain genetic traits in populations. While humans do pass on their genetic heritage, they also pass on a cultural heritage, as the cumulative transmission of experience from generation to generation. Humans can adapt by changing their environment to suit their needs and retain structures over generations. While birds evolved flight through genetic changes, humans could create planes.

Based on the science, we can find that humanity has much in common

---

[5] Richard E. Green, Johannes Krause, Susan E. Ptak, Adrian W. Briggs, Michael T. Ronan, Jan F. Simons, Lei Du, Michael Egholm, Jonathan M. Rothberg, Maja Paunovic and Svante Pääbo, "Analysis of one million base pairs of Neanderthal DNA," *Nature* 444 (2006): 330-336.
[6] R. E. Green, et al., "A draft sequence of the Neandertal Genome," *Science* 328 (2010): 710-722.

with the rest of creation. We share chemical elements with the earth, being made up of water, carbon, etc. We share biological elements (genes, metabolic pathways, functional processes, etc.) with all other living species. We share a genetic code with all of life on earth (although the code differs slightly from our own mitochondria and mitochondria from other evolutionarily distant species such as yeast). Like other species are a product of our environment and our genes. Nevertheless, we can contribute uniquely to the planet, through creativity, language, responsibility, and love. We are the part of creation that contemplates, the part of creation that looks up.

2. How did we get here?

Human history is tied up with our evolution, which is the story of our birth as a species. There are theological questions that are raised as a part of our evolution. At what point in our evolution did pre-humans become human? When did humans acquire a soul? How can we explore Eden in light of our evolution? These are all questions that interface the science with theological issues.

Let us start by discussing evolution and defining evolution. Theodosius Dobzhansky was an evolutionary biologist from Harvard who tried to put evolution in context. He wrote, "Let me try to make crystal clear what is established beyond reasonable doubt, and what needs further study, about evolution. Evolution as a process that has always gone on in the history of the earth can be doubted only by those who are ignorant of the evidence or are resistant to evidence, owing to emotional blocks or to plain bigotry. By contrast, the mechanisms that bring evolution about certainly need study and clarification. There are no alternatives to evolution as history that can withstand critical examination. Yet we are constantly learning new and important facts about evolutionary mechanisms."[7] These thoughts reflect the fact that evolution is the underlying principle in biology even if there is some discussion about mechanisms of how evolution functions.

Darwin's original model of evolution defined biological evolution

---

[7] Theodosius Dobzhansky, "Nothing in Biology Makes Sense Except in the Light of Evolution," *American Biology Teacher* 35 (March 1973), reprinted in *Evolution versus Creationism*, ed. J. Peter Zetterberg (Phoenix AZ: ORYX Press, 1983).

as descent with modification. This definition encompasses small-scale evolution (changes in gene frequency in a population from one generation to the next) and large-scale evolution (the descent of different species from a common ancestor over many generations). The process of evolution is perhaps best defined by Futuyama in his textbook *Evolutionary Biology*: "In the broadest sense, evolution is merely change, and so is all-pervasive; galaxies, languages, and political systems all evolve. Biological evolution ... is change in the properties of populations of organisms that transcend the lifetime of a single individual. The ontogeny of an individual is not considered evolution; individual organisms do not evolve. The changes in populations that are considered evolutionary are those that are inheritable via the genetic material from one generation to the next. Biological evolution may be slight or substantial; it embraces everything from slight changes in the proportion of different alleles within a population (such as those determining blood types) to the successive alterations that led from the earliest protoorganism to snails, bees, giraffes, and dandelions."[8]

Darwin's original model for evolution included a common ancestry for life on earth and noted that speciation occurs through variation in form; Darwin did not know about mutations at his time, but we can now understand these variations as mutations in particular genes. Natural selection selects the variations that are most successful to reproduce in a particular environment. This idea became known as "survival of the fittest" and is the driver for speciation. In this model, extinction is inevitable. In fact, when Darwin published his diagram of a tree of life in *On the Origin of Species*, he showed many branches as dead ends because those species died out and became extinct.[9]

There has been a movement in recent years to represent the "tree of life" in new circular format. This is done because the tree diagram suggests that some organisms are higher than others, while the circular type of diagram shows the relatedness of all organisms and yet at the same time does not try to prioritize which organisms are more important or more highly developed

---

[8] Douglas J. Futuyma, *Evolutionary Biology* (Sunderland, MA: Sinauer Associates, 1997), 751.

[9] Charles Darwin, *On the Origin of Species by Means of Natural Selection, or the Preservation of Favoured Races in the Struggle for Life*, 1st ed. (London: John Murray, 1859); Carles Darwin, *The Descent of Man, and Selection in Relation to Sex*, 1st ed. (London: John Murray, 1871)

than others.[10] From these studies of genetics, we know that the following are true:

- The more related two organisms are, the more alike their gene sequences are; the more distant two organisms are, the more unlike their genetic sequences are.

- In most cases, comparative gene sequencing provided support for standard taxonomical methods for determining relatedness of different organisms.

- Similarities among species are explained by genetic similarities; differences are explained by genetic divergence.

- Species that have evolved special features that adapt them for their evolutionary niche often have rudimentary organs that are reminiscent of their origin—tail bone and "wisdom teeth" in humans, for example

The availability of DNA sequences of complete genomes of man, and other organisms (from primates to plants and bacteria) allows testing of numerous hypotheses based on evolutionary theory and exploration of possible mechanisms of evolution. Nevertheless, evolution is the unifying Theory of biology.[11]

Based on all of the science, then, it is important that we go back and reflect on the Biblical story of Eden and how we might understand it in light of the evolutionary origin of humanity. One modern theologian who attempted to tackle this issue was Sergius Bulgakov, a theologian from the Russian school who taught at the St. Sergius Institute in Paris in the early 20th century. Bulgakov considered the story of Eden to be a hyper-history that explains a truth beyond truth. He wrote that "To assert that the stories [of Genesis] are 'history' in the very same sense as empirical history is to do

---

[10] Wikipedia, List of Sequenced Eukaryotic Genomes, List of Sequenced Bateria, List of Sequenced Archaea, Accessed 20 April 2012.

[11] Gayle E. Woloschak, *Beauty and Unity in Creation: The Evolution of Life* (Minneapolis, MN: Light and Life Publishing Co., 1996); Gayle E. Woloschak, "The compatibility of the principles of evolution with Eastern Orthodoxy," *St. Vladimir's Theological Quarterly* 55 (2011): 209-231.

violence to their direct meaning, to subject them to critical mutilation…"[12]

Bulgakov also considered that Eden was an expression of something yet to be in time, something in the eschaton. He wrote:

> The stumbling block for contemporary thought … is that the history of the world preserves traces neither of Eden nor of the perfection of the original man, which is why the biblical story is considered only a naïve legend … What should one's attitude be toward this story in the face of the existing critique? One can say that the remembrance of an edenic state and of God's garden is nevertheless preserved in the secret recesses of our self-consciousness, as an obscure anamnesis of another being…[13]

In many different traditions, there is a "remembrance" of things that are coming in the future. For example, in the Orthodox tradition, during Liturgy we remember not only the events that occurred in Christ's life, but we also remember His second coming, His judgment of the earth, and more. Bulgakov places Eden in the future, and considers that we each have embedded in our hearts a "remembrance" of something yet to come, the Eden for which humans are intended.

What are the implications of this biology of evolution for human beings and for our planet as a whole? (1) Many of the ancient Church teachers considered that creation is constant and on-going, perhaps even eternal.[14] This fits well with evolutionary theory. (2) Many physicists note that the physics at the moment of the Big Bang are different than the physics we experience today. Most biologists accept that biological laws may have been different when life first evolved than they are now; these conclusions suggest that natural laws are not totally fixed and may change with time. (3) Extinction is natural and occurs as part of evolution. Nevertheless, the rate of extinction occurring now as a result of human-made causes is much higher than that

---

[12] Sergei Bulgakov, *The Bride of the Lamb*, trans. Boris Jakim (Grand Rapids, MI: Eerdmans, 2002), 170.

[13] Ibid, 178

[14] St. Basil the Great, *Hexaemeron Nicene and Post-Nicene Fathers,* Vol. 6, eds. Philip Schaff and Henry Wace (Grand Rapids, MI: Eerdmans, 1952), 52-107. This is also discussed in the book Daniel Buxhoveden and Gayle E. Woloschak, eds., *Science and the Eastern Orthodox Church* (Burlington, VT: Ashgate Publishing Company, 2011).

from more natural causes. The fact that extinction is natural and that the life/death cycle is necessary for evolution does not mean that human-made extinctions should be accepted and be considered to be appropriate.[15]

3. What is normal?

The third question I would like to address is what is normal. The genome sequencing project which set out to sequence the entire human genome resulted in what most people believed was a sequence of a "normal" DNA sequence. These studies revealed that there are many single base pair differences when comparing people in the human population. With so many variations, the question of what is "normal" and what is "disease" has become very difficult to define. For example, when one examines the genes coding for A-B-O blood types, there are differences. The A allele has a longer protein sequence then the B allele. A single base pair change converts the A allele into the O allele. Which one is normal? If we take this question further we can discover many minor differences from one person to another that are encoded for by genetic changes. It is difficult to discern what is the "normal" and what is the mutation. Every difference is a mutation, but when its frequency is high enough in the population it becomes an allele.

Perhaps one of the most interesting examples of gene mutations is one mutation associated with the development of sickle cell anemia. This disease involves a mutation in the gene that encodes the beta-globin protein, the protein that carries oxygen in all our blood. If a person is born with two mutant copies then they will die of sickle cell anemia. If the person has two normal copies of the beta-globin gene then in the United States they would live a normal life span. What is interesting is that when scientists explored the distribution of the sickle cell gene, they found a high frequency in regions in Africa and in the Mediterranean where malaria is very common. Scientists have found that people with one normal copy and one mutant copy of the beta-globin gene are resistant to malaria and yet do not die of sickle cell anemia. This suggests that in regions with malaria there is an advantage to having the mutant beta-globin gene in the human population. In Africa and

---

[15] Gayle E. Woloschak, "God of Life: Contemplating Evolution, Ecology, Extinction," *Ecumenical Review* 65, no. 1 (March 2013): 145-159.

other areas around the Mediterranean Sea, people with two normal copies of the beta globin gene die of malaria with greater frequency than those with one mutant copy of the gene. The advantage to having the mutant copy of the beta-globin gene in the human population is that it permitted some people to survive malaria.[16]

This is an example of a clear relationship between evolution and ecology where selection for survival in the presence of malaria-carrying mosquitoes depended on the presence of the mutant beta-globin gene. Which of these beta-globin genes then is normal? Is it the gene that confers sickle-cell anemia when present in two mutant copies, or is it the gene that protects against malaria when present in one mutant? This example is one that makes us question the use of the word normal and abnormal. Can there be other examples of mutant genes that confer some advantage to humans in other pop environmental situations? Can there be some advantage for example for mutant cystic fibrosis genes, or mutants of the BRCA2 genes that are associated with breast and ovarian cancer?

Some studies have gone so far as to identify genes for left-handedness. This gene is called the LRRTM1 gene, and it regulates which parts of the brain control specific functions such as speech and emotion.[17] Which configuration of the brain is normal? Is it the left oriented brain, which makes people be right-handed, or is it the right oriented brain that makes people be left-handed? Again, what is normal in this situation, and what is abnormal?

The question about what is normal becomes even more important when we think about psychological and social disorders in the genes involved in them. These processes are often hard to define, and the disorders are often multi-genic. Much work will be needed to explore whether gene changes associated with psychological disorders are simple polymorphisms or whether they are disease-inducing mutations. In all cases, the importance of evolutionary selection is paramount.

Despite all of these genetic and scientific conclusions, perhaps we

---

[16] Ana Ferreira, et al., "Sickle Hemoglobin Confers Tolerance to Plasmodium Infection," *Cell* 145 (2011): 398-409.

[17] Clyde Francks, et al., "LRRTM1 on chromosome 2p12 is a maternally suppressed gene that is associated paternally with handedness and schizophrenia," *Molecular Psychiatry* 12 (2007): 1129-1139.

as human beings are called upon to look at ourselves in a way beyond the science. It is interesting that Patriarch Ignatius of Antioch described a hermit who gives little cups of milk to poisonous snakes for them to drink. As Ignatius notes, "he [the monk] knows the snakes in a different way than the scientist."[18]

---

[18] Quoted in the booklet "Towards Life Transfigured" by the Orthodox Fellowship of the Transfiguration.

2. Humans in Light of Epigenetics and Environment

The second series of talks on the topic "becoming human" is about human beings in the context of our epigenetics and our environment. It encompasses questions that are defined in each of the sections below.

1. Nature or nurture?

We know that for many complex human traits our genetics plays at least some role in their expression. Among these traits are right or left handedness, hand clasping patterns, arm folding preferences, the ability to move one's ears, tongue curling, folding, and rolling, musical perfect pitch, homosexuality, a tendency for alcoholism, and many others. The question of how much of who we are as human beings is due to genetics, and how much is due to environment, has plagued biologists for decades. Among these questions are such significant issues as: how much criminal behavior is genetic? How much of our personality is genetic? Are we meant to overcome our environmental shortcomings? Are we made to overcome our genetic shortcomings? In light of genetics, what is sin? Do we believe in behavioral determinism?

A great deal of human behavioral genetics is involved in studying the relative contributions of genetics and environment to individual variations in human behavior. However, behavior is a term that is difficult to quantitate. Endpoints such as IQ or memory cannot be simply associated with specific behaviors. Because behaviors are complex and their genetic background involves multiple genes, it is necessary to analyze families and populations over generations. From broad biological studies we know that some behaviors are species specific, that they breed true in a species or even a strain of organisms, and that they can change in response to environmental stresses, such as brain trauma, drugs, alcohol, and others. Biological behaviors often have an evolutionary history that persists across related species. For example, we humans share social behaviors, nurturing, cooperation, altruism, and even some facial expressions with chimpanzees.[19]

First we will examine behaviors in a few selected animal species, and then we will turn to studies done in humans in order to examine the "nature or nurture" question. Some of the earliest studies on alcohol sensitivity were done in Drosophila, the common fruit fly. The natural habitat of the fruit fly includes fermenting plants where alcohol content can be as much as 3% of the total volume. Some fruit fly strains isolated in the wild have been shown to be resistant to alcohol toxicity. In the laboratory, numerous scientists have carried out a selection process to obtain flies that are resistant to high alcohol levels by processing them through instruments that have gradients of alcohol. These instruments are called inebriators, with low concentrations of alcohol at the top and higher concentrations at the bottom. Fruit flies are placed in the top of the instrument and as they move down to the bottom, those flies that are more resistant to alcohol remain alive and functional. The purpose of these studies is to relate genes from the fly to genes in the human that might play a role in alcoholism. These studies showed that there were several genes that were disrupted or mutated in fruit flies that had alcohol resistance compared to those that were alcohol sensitive. These genes encoded proteins that are important in phosphorylating other proteins. Interestingly, studies in humans showed that some alcoholics exhibited abnormalities in the same metabolic pathways as the resistant fruit flies.[20]

Studies in behavioral genetics have impacted our society greatly in recent years. There has been a resurgence in behavioral determinism, the belief that genetics is the major factor in determining behavior. Based on this

[19] Marc Breedlove, *Biological psychology: an introduction to behavioral, cognitive, and clinical neuroscience,* 5th ed. (Sunderland, MA: Sinauer Associates, 2007).

[20] Ulrike Heberlein, "Genetics of alcohol-induced behaviors in Drosophila," *Alcohol Research & Health* 24, no. 2 (2000): 185-188; Carol M. Singh and Ulrike Heberlein, "Genetic control of acute ethanol-induced behaviors in Dropsophilia," *Alcoholism: Clinical and Experimental Research* 24, no. 8 (2000): 1127-1136.

thinking, many people have considered that there should be genetic testing for criminality, alcoholism, or even homosexuality. This type of thinking is often misplaced and overly simplified. From the scientific perspective it is hard to exclude non-genetic causes in almost any condition, but it is also hard to derive endpoints for a particular condition. There are also some theological questions that come to mind when one considers behavior and genetics. These include:

- If behavior is genetic, then how do we consider sin? How do we define sin in the light all possible genetic inheritance of bad traits?

- As technologies become more easily available for sequencing individuals, are there ethical limits on how these results can be applied?

- How can we explain the existence of "bad" genes if creation is good?

In addition to the fruit fly studies, many other animals were studied for behavior in the quest for genes that might influence human behavior. Perhaps the most recent work that has the caught the interest of the broad population comes from the dog genome project. The goal of this massive effort is to sequence the genomes from many different dog breeds and try to relate particular genetics with different behaviors. For example, it is known that Australian sheep dogs will herd small children in the absence of sheep to herd. The Doberman pincher is known to have a compulsive behavior of sucking on its flank, and it is thought that this is similar to obsessive-compulsive behavior in humans. The identification of genes associated with these behaviors may point to similar genes in humans that are associated with obsessive compulsive disorders.[21] To date, eighty-five different breeds of dogs have been sequenced and analyzed. Those studies have shown that dogs are remarkably similar genetically despite they are diverse appearances. The diversity in dogs is lower than the diversity that is found among humans, mice, or rats, but is similar to the genetic diversity found in other domestic animals.[22]

---

[21] Nicholas H. Dodman, et al., "A canine chromosome 7 locus confers compulsive disorder susceptibility," *Molecular Psychiatry* 15 (2010): 8-10.

[22] Heidi G. Parker, "Genetic structure of the purebred domestic dog," *Science* 304, no. 5674 (2004): 1160-1164; Heidi G. Parker, et al., "An expressed Fgf4 retrogene is associated with breed-defining chondrodysplasia in domestic dogs," *Science* 325, no. 5943 (2009): 995.

There are two reflections on this interface between genetics and religion that represents different poles. First I would like to draw attention to Paul Evdokimov who is concerned that science and genetics may be siding against God. Evdokimov wrote:

> Humanity risks being reduced to rationally conditioned, predictable gestures, with its critical faculties, cunningly controlled or inhibited. A balanced interaction between material progress and spiritual growth seems more and more problematic. An existence that has broken away from God is built on the refusal of God. Science, good in itself, risks finding itself set up entirely against God.[23]

This first reflection gives us a cautionary view, and while not opposed to science, warns that there can be dangers associated with embracing scientific thought to the exclusion of the spiritual.

At the other end of the spectrum is the Romanian theologian Staniloae who wrote:

> Science also serves to increase the human beings spiritual growth, for it can uncover the apophatic meaning of the world, hidden in God, on an even higher level, just as it can also glean that meaning from the experience of human history. These latter, if they are good spirit dances, extend human communion.[24]

Staniloae is more optimistic about science and its possibilities for bringing about an enhanced relationship among human beings and humans with God.

2. How much does epigenetics contribute to who we are?

Our next question deals with how much epigenetics contributes to who we are as human beings. Before we examine this issue, we must define epigenetics. Epigenetics is the study of changes in cellular phenotype caused

---

[23] Paul Evdokimov, *The Sacrament of Love*, trans. Anthony P. Gythiel and Victoria Steadman (Crestwood, NY: St. Vladimir's Seminary Press, 1985).

[24] Dumitru Staniloae, *The Experience of God*, trans. Ioan Ionita and Robert Barringer (Brookline, MA: Holy Cross Orthodox Press, 1994), 102.

by mechanisms other than changes in the underlying DNA sequences. Examples include cellular differentiation, DNA methylation, and chromatin remodeling. Multiple epigenetic effects have been identified in human beings. One of the most important epigenetic changes is called imprinting, which involves situations when the father and mother each contribute different epigenetic patterns for specific genomic loci in their germ cells.[25] Thus, even if the genetic sequences are the same, one or the other of parental genes will be the only one to function in the next generation. In humans, over thirty genes have been identified that are regulated by imprinting, the process of inheriting a gene from both parents by having only one expressed in the offspring.[26] Transgenerational epigenetic effects have been identified crossing more than one generation. Even epigenetic carcinogens have been identified; these cause an increase in tumor frequency, but have no mutagenic activity. Epigenetic carcinogens include arsenites, nickel, diethylstilbestrol, and others.

One of the mechanisms important in epigenetics includes DNA methylation, which occurs on C residues in the DNA. Genes that are turned off even when they should not be often have C residues with methyl residues added to them; genes that are turned on usually have no methyl groups on their C residues. Alterations that last less than one cell cycle do not qualify as being epigenetic under the strict definition.

Another example of epigenetic regulation in humans is one that is well known in the scientific literature, the process of X chromosome inactivation. In humans and other mammals, each female inherits one of the X chromosomes from each parent. Nevertheless, in each cell of the mature female one X chromosome is used and one is inactivated. The choice of which X chromosome is inactivated appears to be random, leading to differential gene expression from one cell to another. A prime example of X inactivation is the calico cat. In cats, genes on the X chromosome encode for orange and black colors of fur. In female cats that are calico, the orange

---

[25] Adrian Bird, "Perceptions of epigenetics," *Nature* 447 (May 2007): 396-398; *Nature Insight: Epigenetics* 447: 396-440, supplemental issue devoted to epigenetics; Database volume 9, issues 5-6 special issue devoted to epigenetics, 2010.

[26] N. Carolyn Schanen, "Epigenetics of autism spectrum disorders," *Human Molecular Genetics* 15 (2006): R138-R150.

gene is inactivated in some cells and the black gene is inactivated in others. Male cats have only one X chromosome, which is never inacativated. Calico cats result from X inactivation in females and one never identifies any calico male cats.[27]

One of the most interesting stories allowing us to examine epigenetic effects in humans is the study of identical and fraternal twins. Identical twins have identical genomes, and they are natural clones of each other while fraternal twins represent siblings who are born at the same time. Minnesota did large numbers of twins studies comparing identical twins raised together and raised apart as well as fraternal twins raised together and raised apart. These studies showed many interesting aspects associated with genetics and epigenetics of humans. They found differences in disease spectrum among twins examining such diseases as different cancers, psychological diseases, Alzheimer disease, and others. These results all point to a role for either environment and/or epigenetics in the disease process. At the same time some traits expected to have a divergence among identical twins did not. These include selection of clothing, first names for children, furniture in the home, and many others, implying that there may be a role for genetics in choices that we make.

Some traits that were shown to have concordance between both identical twins and fraternal twins included alcoholism and memory skills. Many others showed a concordance among identical twins but not among fraternal twins including general intelligence, verbal reasoning, and scholastic achievement. Other traits that showed no concordance among fraternal twins and only a slight at best concordance among identical twins include schizophrenia, autism, spatial reasoning, and reading disability. This study noted, "on multiple measures of personality and temperament, occupational and leisure time interests and social attitudes, identical twins reared apart are about as similar as identical twins reared together. Interestingly most of these studies did not take epigenetics into consideration and environment is

---

[27] Janice J. Ahn and J. T. Lee, "X Chromosome: X Inactivation," *Nature Education* 1, no. 1 (2008); Christian P. Bacher, et al., "Transient colocalization of X-inactivation centres accompanies the initiation of X inactivation," *Nature Cell Biology* 8, (2006): 293-299; Peter Fraser and Wendy Bickmore, "Nuclear organization of the genome and the potential for gene regulation," *Nature* 447 (2007): 413-417.

certainly a confounder in these studies."[28]

Several recent studies have examined the question of why twins age differently. Comparisons of photographs of identical twins in their late years often show differences that were not apparent in their youth. The reasons for these differences are not understood, but point to a role for epigenetics and also environment in determining some aspects of who we are as human beings.[29]

3. Where are we going as humans?

This final question in a set of three about the genetics and environment takes us to the issue of technology, and how far we plan to take technology as human beings. Modern technologies are providing us with tools to manipulate single cells, genomes, and, as a result, humanity. There is a rapid movement from technology to discovery, making it hard to limit the technology itself. Most limitation is at the level of the application of the technology, and not at the development of it. For most technologies, there are positive and negative aspects to it, and decisions about what our right and wrong uses revolve around the application itself.

Most fields of science are hardly technology driven, and the discovery of new technologies drastically impacts the science that can be done. Often there is a division between those that have the technology and those that do not have it. In general, those scientists that don't explore new technologies rapidly become obsolete in their fields.[30] One need only look at the development of polymerase chain reaction (PCR) technologies to see how rapidly an entire field of study can be changed by one technique. Prior to the use of PCR, analyses of DNA in cells required bulky cultures of over 1 million cells.

---

[28] Susan L. Farber, *Identical Twins Reared Apart: A Reanalysis*, (New York: Basic Books, 1981); J. Joseph, *The Gene Illusion: Genetic Research in Psychiatry and Psychology Under the Microscopy*, (New York: Algora, 2003); T. J. Bouchard Jr., et al., "Source of Human Psychological Differences: The Minnesota Study of Twins Reared Apart," *Science* 250 (1990): 223-228; William G. Iacono and Matt McGue, "Minnesota Twin Family Study," *Twin Research* 5 (2002): 283-487.

[29] Jean-Sebastien Doucet and Albert H. C. Wong, "Monozygotic twins and epigenetics," in *Epigenetic Regulation and Epigenomics*, ed. Robert A. Meyers (Hoboken, NJ: Wiley-Blackwell, 2012); Trygve O. Tollefsbol, ed., *Epigenetics of Aging*, (London: Springer, 2009).

[30] Gayle E. Woloschak, "Technology: Life and Death, Orthodoxy in Korea," *110th Anniversary of Orthodox Witness in Korea* (2010): 67-81 (in Korean, 55-66).

The discovery of PCR allowed for the same types of analyses to be done on a single cell. This meant that archival samples, forensic samples, tissue biopsies, and other samples with cells present in limiting amounts could now be studied at the DNA level. In biology and other scientific fields, new types of microscopy such as atomic force microscopy and x-ray microscopy have revolutionized materials sciences and nanotechnology; scientists without access to these capabilities are limited in the types of work that they can conduct.

New technologies are providing us with tools to manipulate the environment, nature, energy, food, our new genomes, and more. Market demands make it difficult to limit the technology, resulting in a rapid movement from discovery to implementation. Safety issues associated with technology are not well discussed in the broad media, nor in the scientific community, and if they are discussed it is not done in a timely manner. On the other hand, there is a conviction among the general public that technology can heal all things afflicting humanity. Sometimes a belief in technology even supersedes a belief in God. There is little pause for reflection in public about whether a technology should be used, and often novelty may suffice to drive a new technology to market.[31]

In the scientific realm, we can see examples of technology drastically changing approaches to medical questions. For example, structural biology has given us the structures of proteins and this has in turn led to rational drug design and the development of new therapeutic agents. Gene technology and proteomics have identified the causes of many human diseases, allowing for rapid screening for the same diseases, but also making genetic counseling available. Reproductive technologies such as in vitro fertilization, stem cell research, and cloning have allowed for treatment of human reproductive disorders and may lead to therapeutic interventions for a variety of different human diseases. Finally, nanotechnology offers the promise of manipulating organisms on the level of single cells, sending nano sized constructs into the cell to fix disorders such as cancer, diabetes, and others.[32]

---

[31] Gayle E. Woloschak, "What is on the Holizon? What is Science Likely to be Doing in the Upcoming Years?," in *Theological Foundations in an Age of Biological Intervention*, ed. David C. Ratke, (Minneapolis, MN: Lutheran University Press, 2007), 25-40.

[32] Gayle E. Woloschak, "Nanotechnology: Small Times are Upon Us," *Journal of Lutheran Ethics*

It is interesting to note that of all the fields of science, religious communities have had a large impact on stem cell studies and beginning of life technologies. When initial experiments with stem cells were done, scientists were open to using all sources for possible stem cells including an aborted fetus. When religious communities expressed their concern, scientists were driven to finding alternative sources of stem cells including efforts to coax adult cells to revert to an embryonic state and using cells in the amniotic fluid as stem cells. These examples have met with variable success, but nevertheless have shown the importance that religious communities can play in driving scientific approaches.[33]

One area of science and technology that is becoming more and more important is the use of biological enhancement.[34] There are websites that offer to make people become "more than human: altering minds, bodies, and lifespans through technology." Some technologies are anticipated to improve health, but others seek to improve the healthy. As one example a team of investigators was looking for a cure for Alzheimer's disease trying to improve response times in mice. They never realized that their work may have military applications and could be used to improve the response times of soldiers. Another team of investigators developed tools to aid the paralyzed such as moving a cursor on a computer screen just by thinking about it. While this is very useful for the paralyzed again military applications could be of some concern when a soldier can drop a bomb or fire a gun by just thinking about it.

---

6 (February 2006).

[33] Nadya Lumelsky, et al., "Differentiation of embryonic stem cells to insulin-secreting structures similar to pancreatic islets," *Science* 292, no. 5520 (2001): 1389; Jon S. Odorico, et al., "Multilineage differentiation from human embryonic stem cell lines," *Stem Cells* 19, no. 3 (2001): 193; Rajeswari Ravichandran, et al., "Effects of nanotopography on stem cell phenotypes," *World J Stem Cells* 1, no.1 (2009): 55; Keisuke Okita, et al., "Generation of germline-competent induced pluripotent stem cells," *Nature* 448, no. 7151 (2007): 313-17; Hongyan Zhou, et al., "Generation of Induced Pluripotent Stem Cells Using Recombinant Proteins," *Cell Stem Cell* 4, no. 5 (2009): 381.

[34] Francis Futuyama, *Our Posthuman Future: Consequences of the Biotechnology Revolution,* (New York: Farrar Straus and Giroux, 2002); Enita A. Williams, *Good, Better, Best: The Human Quest for Enhancement, ed.* Mark S. Frankel. Summary Report of an Invitational Workshop. Convened by the Scientific Freedom, Responsibility and Law Program. American Association for the Advancement of Science. June 1–2, 2006.

We know now that many drugs are used to improve attention in students with Attention Deficit Disorder; there is concern that the drugs such as Ritalin can be used to improve performance on exams, and in fact in many colleges today it is known that students take the drug prior to taking a test. Use of prosthetics, robotics, and artificial intelligence blurs the boundaries between the human body and information processing machines. While so far there has been no direct intervention at the level of the human genome (that is, at the level of the eggs or the sperm), there are certainly companies that offer preimplantation genetic screening.[35] These companies use "unnatural selection" to promise parents using in vitro fertilization that they can select for babies with, for example blue eyes, blonde hair, and other specified traits.

There is no question that technology is going to continue to develop at a rapid rate, so rapidly that it will be difficult to regulate it. As noted above, the impact of religious communities has been seeing predominantly at the level of regulation but in general it is very limited in its influence. Biotechnologies increase the number of decisions and turning points in life. In the past when a couple was childless, the decision to be made was whether to adopt or not; now, couples must decide whether to have in vitro fertilization or not, whether to have a surrogate mother or not, whether they will use donor sperm or the father's sperm, etc. Often when people require advice and turn to their pastors, ministers, rabbis, and other leaders of the religious communities to help them in this decision-making process; it is a challenge for pastors to be equipped with sufficient understanding and insight to help individuals, couples, and families address these issues. Even if seminaries were to have classes in science and scientific approaches, those would become rapidly outdated as the pastor spent more time past his or her graduating years. What is the solution to this problem? There is a need for stronger collaboration between pastors and those in their communities that can provide information on these issues. The use of pastoral teams in religious communities that might include in addition to the pastor other trained individuals such as physicians, nurses, scientists, engineers, etc., can be used to help address each of these types of issues as they come up. For example a team considering eco-friendly

<hr>

[35] Alan R. Thornhill, et al., "ESHRE PGD Consortium 'Best practice guidelines for clinical preimplantation genetic diagnosis (PGD) and preimplantation genetic screening (PGS)'," *Human Reproduction* 20 (January 2005): 35-48.

changes in a community might include the pastor, an engineer, a scientist, a construction worker, and others. This broad team approach to pastoring is needed in today's world where most projects are interdisciplinary.[36]

It is important to acknowledge that all knowledge is derived from divine sources. Basil the Great in his greater rule number fifty-five noted the following about medicine as a gift from God: "Medicine is a gift from God even if some people do not make the right use of it. Granted, it would be stupid to put all hope of a cure in the hands of doctors, yet there are people who stubbornly refuse their help altogether." And later, Basil similarly notes, "All the different sciences and techniques have been given to us by God to make up for the deficiencies of nature.... Not by chance does the earth produce plants that have healing properties. It is clearly evident that the Creator wants to give them to us to use."[37] As Basil states scientific knowledge is a gift from God, and one of the tasks of humanity is to be able to know how to use it, when to use it, and when to just let things be. This requires discernment, where knowledge may be gained from cooperation of theologians and clergy with scientists, philosophers, historians, and others. Nevertheless, discernment of the situation and what is proper must come from something deeper than simple ethics; it must be derived from a spiritual awareness of the world and of the self.

Discernment needs to weigh its answers on a fine scale. Anthony Bloom, theologian writing in the 20th century remarked: "Our task is not merely to imitate what was done by the Saints of previous eras, but somehow to appropriate at a much deeper level the way in which they engage their own historical environment, seeking to respond as they would've responded had they lived in our day."[38] This is the task that faces us – trying to take principles that we hold strong and dear and applying them to the problems that face us in today's world.

---

[36] Gayle E. Woloschak, "Contemporary Bioethical Issues for Orthodox Christians," *Praxis* 9 (2010): 13-15; Gayle E. Woloschak, "Technology: How Far is Too far?," *Again* 29 (2007): 7-9.
[37] Quoted in Gayle E. Woloschak, "Stem Cells, Cloning, and Other Matters," *The Handmaiden* (2005): 28.
[38] Metropolitan Anthony Bloom, final encyclical, www.masarchive.org

3. Reflections on Personhood

This final talk will focus on the human person and on personhood, providing a theological and practical discussion on how personhood leads to particular attributes that are distinctly human.

1. What is personhood?

In Greek theology there is a distinction between the idea of a person (from the Greek word prosopon) and the concept of the substance that underlies what the person is (defined in the Greek word hypostasis). Prosopon was the face or mask that was used in Greek theater where actors on stage wore masks to reveal their character and emotional state to the audience. This concept of the revealing mask usually includes some sort of manifestation of the self that includes one's inner thoughts and feelings. Alternatively, the word hypostasis was used to describe the substance of the person, the underlying reality of the person, what that person actually is in their essence. Both terms were much discussed by John Zizioulas, an Orthodox theologian from Greece whose book called *Being as Communion* has been very influential.

Zizioulas contends that a person develops in context of and in communion with others, but that forms of communion that deny or suppress the person in any way is wrong. He uses the idea of the prosopon as the mask from ancient Greek theater and notes that these plays and characters first led to the idea of humans as persons because in the theater audiences witnessed conflicts between human freedom and necessity worked out in dramatic form. In Greek theater the human strives to become a person, to rise up against that which oppresses him, whether it be the gods, his fate, or everyday life. To

Zizioulas, the idea of personhood ties the human with relationship, with the ability to form associations, and ultimately (in Greek theater) with the ability to organize life into a nation-state. Uniqueness is something absolute with a person, and there are no two persons who are identical. Zizioulas writes: "the goal of personhood is the person itself; personhood is the total fulfillment of being, the Catholic (universal) expression of its nature…. Diffused today throughout all forms of social life is the intense search for personal identity. The person is not relativized without provoking a reaction."[39]

According to Zizioulas, the essence of personhood can be divided into two types of relationships. 1. The hypostasis of biological existence – this is constituted by a person's conception and birth and earthly existence; the person is the product of the communion between two people and it is rooted in creativeness. This biological existence is tied to biological needs that form around relationships among people. 2. The hypostasis of otherworldliness – this existence is based on uncreated existence, and comes "from above". This personhood is rooted in the person's relationship to God. Biological existence can become utterly selfish and based in egotism in the absence of some form of experiential existence that goes beyond the creaturely existence. These two hypostases are related to each other, and certainly the person's relationship with others is tied to the person's relationship with God.[40] Zizioulas sums up how this idea of personhood fits in with models of evolution in the following way:

> The belief in human superiority received a blow from Darwinism when Charles Darwin proved that not only humans but also animals although to a lesser degree, are capable of thinking. So if the human is in the image of God, this must be due to other capabilities than his/her ability to think, and it is these capabilities which we must learn to value.[41]

This reflection brings us to our next question about what is unique about humanity and human persons.

---

[39] John Zizioulas, *Being as Communion: Studies in Personhood and the Church* (Crestwood, NY: St. Vladimir's Seminary Press, 1985), 47.

[40] John Zizioulas, *Communion and Otherness*, ed. Paul McPartlan, (London: T and T Clark, 2006); John D. Zizioulas, *Eucharist, Bishop, Church*, trans. Elizabeth Theokritoff (Brookline, MA: Holy Cross Orthodox Press, 2001).

[41] John Zizioulas, *Being as Communion*, 87.

2. What is unique about human persons?

There have been numerous dialogues over the years about what makes humans unique compared to other species, particularly in light of the fact that we are all animals and part of the animal kingdom. Some have suggested that it is the development of culture that makes us unique, and while one can argue that many animals have cultures including birds, chimpanzees and others, those cultures are not passed on to future generations in the same ways that human cultures are. Human language is also uniquely developed. While birds sing and other species communicate by sounds, human language allows for the development of relationships that lead to personhood. If we consider comments mentioned earlier about the Greek theater, we note that some aspects of being a person include expressions of emotion and of personal freedom that is unique for the person; language is one parameter that permits us to do this.

The Darwinian concept of "survival of the fittest" is based predominantly on genetic heritage, the survival that comes through particular DNA sequences and particular genes. With regard to genetic heritage, evolution operates at the level of populations and their genes and selects for the most reproductively fit populations. Nevertheless, humans also have a cultural and technological heritage that is the cumulative transmission of knowledge and experience from one generation to the next, aiding in the survival of humans as a species. Humans can adapt by changing their environment to suit their needs, and they can re-create their niche without the need to wait for evolution to select for the traits that are best suited for that environment. Birds had to evolve flight through genetic changes; humans could create planes in order to fly. Francisco Ayala made this point in the following quote:

> Biological inheritance is based on the transmission of genetic information, in humans by much the same as in other sexually reproducing organisms. But cultural inheritance is distinctively human, based on transmission of information by a teaching and learning process, which is, in principle, independent of biological parentage. Cultural inheritance makes possible the cumulative transmission of experience from generation to generation. Cultural heredity is a swifter and more effective (because it can be designed) mode of adaptation to the environment than the

biological mode. The advent of cultural heredity ushered in cultural evolution, which transcends biological evolution.[42]

In my opinion, one thing that sets humans aside from all other animals is our capacity to use language. Humans have the ability for acquiring and using complex systems of communication, and human language relies on social conventions and learning, which has all led to a complicated structure. It is believed that language evolved when early hominids started gradually changing their primate communication systems, acquiring the ability to form a theory of other minds and shared intentionality. The development of language seems to coincide with an increase of brain volume, although it is not certain whether one came before the other or whether they coevolved together. Languages have also been shown to evolve over time.

What makes human language unique from that of animals? Human language is open-ended and productive, allowing for an infinite set of utterances from a finite set of elements. Symbols and grammatical rules are largely arbitrary. Animals are able to use symbols. The bonobo Kanzi was trained in Japan to learn symbolic signs to communicate in a form of sign language. Kanzi was able to learn about the same number of signs that a four-year-old learns.[43] Human language can employ grammatical and semantic categories such as nouns and verbs. Human language is modality independent, that is it can be audible, written, sign language, or tactile (Braille).

In ancient times there were many models that were used to explain the evolution of language; one mural in Mexico from A.D. 200 shows a scroll coming forth from the mouth of a person reflecting that person's speech. In Europe in the 400s, it was believed that each nation was given a language after the tower of Babel, and that each language belongs to the nation as something to safeguard. In the medieval era, many people believe that there existed a language of paradise and that all other languages spread from it; major arguments included whether the original language of paradise was

---

[42] Francisco J. Ayala, "Biology Precedes, Culture Transcends: An Evolutionist's View of Human Nature," *Zygon* 33 (1998): 507-523.

[43] John Mitani, review of *Kanzi: The Ape at the Brink of the Human Mind*, by Sue Savage-Rumbaugh, *Scientific American* 272 (1995); John E. Joseph, Nigel Love & Talbot J. Taylor, *Landmarks in Linguistic Thought II: The Western Tradition in the 20th Century* (London & New York: Routledge, 2001), 219-236.

Latin, Hebrew, German, etc. In the 1700s the tree model came in vogue, which suggested that the descent of languages occurred similar to that of the phylogenetic tree. More recently only two models have been proposed for how language evolved in humans. Chomsky believes that language appeared as a single mutation or change along the hominid tree that eventually led to humans.[44] Most others believe that language developed from animal cognition through continuous development over time. The model for language development used most frequently in the modern literature is considered to be a "genetic relationship" among languages, but this usually means a genealogical relationship.[45]

The relatedness of languages is perhaps best observed when one examines Romance languages and can see that many words are very similar between Latin, French, Italian, and Spanish. Some examples are presented in the table below[46]:

English	Latin	French	Italian	Spanish
thing	causa	chose	cosa	cosa
sing	cantare	chanter	cantare	cantar
horse	caballus	cheval	cavallo	caballo
plant	planta	plante	pianta	llanta
night	noctis	nuit	notte	noche
fact	factum	fait	fatto	hecho
milk	lacte	lait	latte	leche
eight	octo	huit	otto	och

---

[44] Noam Chomsky, *Language and Mind* (New York: Harcourt, Brace & World, 1968); Noam Chomsky, *Current Issues in Linguistic Theory* (The Hague: Mouton, 1964).

[45] Murray Gell-Mann and Merritt Tuhlen, "The Origin of Word Order," *Proceedings of the National Academy of Sciences* 108, no. 42 (2011): 17290-5; Raymond G. Gordon, Jr., ed., *Ethnologue: Languages of the World,* 15th ed. (Dallas, TX: SIL Internatinational, 2005); Merritt Ruhlen, *A guide to the world's languages* (Stanford: Stanford University Press, 1987).

[46] Modified from Wikipedia, Development of languages.

In fact, language trees showing the relatedness of language families of the world support the notion of a genealogical relationship for all languages, and one can identify areas of the world where particular languages dominate and spread, much like evolution.

Many religions place a great significance to language through the use of particular words for worship and prayer, through the use of particular names for God and other deities, and others. In Christianity Christ is called the Logos, a Greek word that can mean word, discourse, or reason. For example John 1:1, states "In the beginning was the Word, and the Word was with God, and the Word was God." This concept of Christ as Logos is frequently tied up with the Old Testament idea of "Sophia" as the wisdom of God.[47]

In the Genesis story of creation, God created by speaking ("… And God said"). This implies a relationship between speaking and creativity, and this may be related to the commonly accepted perspective that people develop new ideas as they are speaking or even as they are interacting with or listening to others. The concept of think tanks has come about from gathering groups of people together to talk about problems and develop solutions; the act of talking, of speaking is expected to be more productive for developing creative ideas than putting individuals in a series of separate locations and asking them to think alone and find a solution to a problem. There is also relationship between speaking and confession.[48] Many therapists working with prisoners have noted that those prisoners who admitted their crimes are on a better road to recovery than those who never admit what they have done. The idea of using speech to unburden ourselves of our problems helps us to work through our concerns.

The story of Genesis provides yet another example of the importance of speaking. Adam was given the task of providing a name for each of the animals. One could ask why was this so, what is the importance of giving a name to something. What are the things that we name? We name our children, we name our pets, some people name their ranches or farms; in general, we

---

[47] Dionysius the Areopagite, *Dionysius the Areopagite on the Divine Names and the Mystical Theology*, trans. Clarence E. Rolt, (Lake Worth, FL: IBIS Press, 2004).

[48] Aristotle Papanikolaou, "Honest to God: Confession and Desire," *Thinking Through Faith*, Aristotle Papanikolaou and Elizabeth Prodromou, eds. (New York: St. Vladimir's Seminary Press, 2008).

name those things for which we are responsible. In my own tradition, Eastern Orthodox Church, the godparent names his or her godchild, which reflects the responsibility of the godparent in the upbringing of the child. The story of Adam naming the animals in Genesis points to the responsibility of humanity for animals and for the earth as a whole; this is reflective of human responsibility for creation. Thus, one can say that the words of God and of humans both create and claim responsibility.

It should also be noted in this Genesis story that as Adam spoke the names of the animals, he learned something about himself. He learned that he was not like them, that there was something that distinguished himself from the animals. At the same time, Adam also learned he was alone. The mere speaking of the names of the animals was a teaching experience for Adam. Bulgakov believes that there is a logical significance to this naming. He wrote:

> The name itself and naming could be considered a human invention existing only for man and in man. The Archangel's Annunciation of the Name of God, which is also a human name, revealed to the world and to humanity that the name of God is and therefore is also a human naming … this imparts to naming a mysterious, profound, and realistic character. This affirmation, namely that the name enters into the image of God in man that it is this image … that constitutes the most profound ontological basis of naming: thought collides here with the power of fact…[49]

While we are talking about speech, we must also realize that there is a profound significance found in the absence of speech or the presence of silence. Silence is often a choice for humans, and it provides us with many opportunities to be aware of ourselves, of others, and of the Other. Often quieting our inner and outer lives allows us listen to God speak. Meditation is used as a means to achieve inner silence, substituting one thought for another. Many religious traditions have used silence as a means of achieving inner peace. Because we humans have language, we can appreciate silence in a different way that other creatures on the planet.[50]

---

[49] Sergius Bulgakov, *Icons and the Name of God,* trans. Boris Jakim (Grand Rapids, MI: William B. Eerdmans Press, 2012).

[50] Metropolitan Hierotheos of Nafpaktos, *A night in the desert of the Holy Mountain,* trans. Effie

3. Is suffering uniquely human?

In this final question we will explore the aspects of human suffering. We must appreciate that pain is distinct from suffering although suffering can involve the perception of pain as something that is occurring and engenders a desire to stop it. Suffering can involve not only physical but also nonphysical emotional components. Do other animals suffer? We know that elephants have death rituals, and that many mammals show some of the psychopathologies that humans do in response to death or serious illness. In fact many antidepressants used for humans are tested in animals first.

Tied up with the question of suffering is the use of technology to reduce suffering. Chemotherapy for instance, was developed to help reduce human suffering from cancer so that the quality of life could be improved and the pain from the disease could be reduced. When modern technological tools were developed, many were offered to the public as tools to free up time allowing humans to explore deeper desires and achieve a closeness to family, friends, and God. Early advertisements in the 1940's and 1950's about washing machines promised that women who purchased and used such a machine would ultimately have more time for their families. Computers were originally marketed as tools for saving a large amount of time in the workplace, allowing workers more time for other needs. Did these technologies ever achieve the goals they had promised? Did they have other side effects? It seems that despite promises to free up time, these technologies have only served to increase humanity's busy-ness.

Is it ever possible, then, to eliminate suffering? To some extent, suffering is connected with death, and fear of suffering is related to the vulnerability of humans and all of life to experience death. Despite this, death is a part of the normal cycle of life on earth, and as we noted in the very first lecture evolution depends upon death. Much of our technology is driven to postpone (or some would dream to eliminate) death. There are some who believe in technology, even more than they believe in God. They hope that technology will solve all of humanity's problems, and therefore keep the human species from destruction. I've heard of many who talk about ecological problems on earth and how there is really no need to worry about conserving resources,

---

Mavromichali (Levadia, Greece: Birth of the Theotokos Monastery, 1991).

because certainly human technology will solve all problems from global warming to lack of energy long before we get to some dangerous tipping point. There are numerous agents that are sold to prevent or postpone signs of aging, poor health, and others.

How do we then understand this world of suffering, disasters, and death? We know that suffering is a requirement of our free will, and certainly we can always choose to do bad and hurt others rather than to choose to do good. Free will is about the ability of a person to make choices free of constraint. God could have constrained humanity, but instead God created humanity to be able to choose freely between good and evil. The result is that while sometimes we choose good, and sometimes we choose bad, we are all affected by those choices. Imagine a world where death never occurred, and leaders like Stalin and Hitler could live forever; a world without death could be a very dangerous place. Kallistos Ware addressed this issue of the ability of humans for good or bad:

> Because the human person is both microcosm and mediator, unifying the creation and offering it back to God in thanksgiving – because more particularly, we humans have the ability consciously and by deliberate choice to modify and refashion the world – there is imposed upon us a daunting responsibility. The fact that we are made in the divine image and so endowed with freedom – creators after the image of God the Creator – carries with it a terrible risk. We can use our creative power both for good and for evil. We can illumine and transfigure, but equally we can pollute and destroy.[51]

Another concept that is related to human suffering involves the development of mental disorders, which are certainly devastating and to some extent poorly understood. Why do mental disorders exist in humans? Some believe that higher cognitive powers in our species could not have evolved without psychological disorders. It is possible that the presence of psychological disease in the human population is genetically linked to higher cognitive powers and that the two go hand-in-hand. Without the potential for psychological disorders, humans may never have evolved cognition. Models

---

[51] Kallistos Ware, *Through the Creation to the Creator* (London: Friends of the Centre, 1997).

about human and Neanderthal evolution indicate that this may be so because they have found that the genes associated with autism, schizophrenia and others are absent from the Neanderthal population, a group thought to have low cognitive skills.

We must also consider why some natural disasters occur, since they are clearly responsible for a large amount of human suffering. We have earthquakes because the continental plates of the earth move; if they did not move, our climate, our environment, our planet, would not be able support life in the same way. The same can be true for most of our weather systems – storms are needed to shape ecosystems, volcanoes are needed for our planet to breathe and be viable. So these natural disasters are associated with our planet's lifecycle are the price we must pay for a planet that supports life as we know it.

Finally, suffering tempers us and helps us grow as individuals. There are so many people who told me over the years that suffering through a disease, a family tragedy, or a particular problem, improved their life very much. I believe this is something that can be understood only with experience. Dostoyevsky who perhaps was the master of describing human suffering said, "Accept suffering and achieve atonement through it – that is what you must do."[52] By the same token he saw that love and suffering go hand-in-hand and that it is not possible to love without suffering. He wrote:

> On our earth we can only love with suffering and through suffering. We cannot love otherwise, and we know of no other sort of love. I want suffering in order to love. I long, I thirst, this very instant, to kiss with tears the earth that I have left, and I don't want, I won't accept life on any other![53]

The issue of suffering cannot be addressed without also reflecting for a moment on the book of Job 38: 4-18. In this passage God talks to Job and says:

> 4 "Where were you when I laid the foundations of the

---

[52] Fyodor Dostoyevsky, *Crime and Punishment*, published originally in 1866, quoted in Wikipedia Fyodor Dostoyevsky.

[53] Fyodor Dostoyevsky, *The Dream of a Ridiculous Man*, published originally in 1877, quote uses the translation of Constance Garnett, 1916.

earth? Tell me, if you have understanding. [5] Who determined its measurements? Surely you know!   Who stretched a measuring line across it? [6] On what were its bases sunk, or who laid its cornerstone— [7] when the morning stars sang together and all the sons of God shouted for joy?

[8] Or who shut up the sea behind doors when it burst forth from the womb, [9] when I made the clouds its garment and thick darkness its swaddling band, [10] and prescribed bounds for it and set its bars and doors, [11] when I said, 'This far shall you come and no farther; here is where your proud waves be stayed'?

[12] "Have you ever given orders to the morning, or shown the dawn its place, [13] that it might take the earth by the edges and shake the wicked out of it? [14] The earth takes shape like clay under a seal; its features stand out like those of a garment. [15] The wicked are denied their light, and their upraised arm is broken.

[16] "Have you journeyed to the springs of the sea or walked in the recesses of the deep? [17] Have the gates of death been shown to you? Have you seen the gates of the deepest darkness? [18] Have you comprehended the vast expanses of the earth? Tell me, if you know all this.

I believe the story of Job is a powerful one, not only because of Job's suffering but also because this story expresses the abyss between human understanding and the complete knowledge of the workings of God. The mystery of God's creation is reflected with detail in Job 38.[54] Through science we may seek to gain knowledge about God's creation, but we must realize the limits of our comprehension and the utter impossibility of applying our cognitive powers to an understanding of God that penetrates to the depth of his being. There is often a tendency among humans to make an idol of all new technologies; nevertheless, there is a need to appreciate that these novelties are not only God-given but also insignificant in the context of God's creation, it's complexities, and its workings. This may also relate to suffering—we

[54] Johanna Manly, *Wisdom, Let us Attend: Job, The Fathers, and the Old Testament* (Menlo Park, CA: Monastery Books, 1997).

human beings may not be able to fully fathom why it is that our species must suffer. This mystery points out the need for humility, particularly in the face of our technology, our knowledge and our understanding.

As my closing thoughts, I would like to explore the word *anthropos*, the Greek word for human. It is derived from the word "anarthrein," which means to look up. Humans, unlike most animals, look up towards heaven. Humans are heavenly, yet earthly; humans are spiritual, yet material. Kallistos Ware expressed the role of humanity well when he said, "Our human task is to be *syndesmos* and *gephyra*, the bond and bridge of God's creation."[55]

---

[55] This idea of humans (anthropos) as the one who "looks up" and contemplates is described by Bishop Kallistos Ware, *Through the Creation to the Creator* (London: Friends of the Centre, 1997), 8.

Homily
Dewfall and Divine Providence

Margaret E. Schott

Hosea 13:1-6

When Ephraim spoke, there was trembling; he was exalted in Israel;
but he incurred guilt through Baal and died.
² And now they keep on sinning and make a cast image for themselves,
idols of silver made according to their understanding,
all of them the work of artisans.
"Sacrifice to these," they say. People are kissing calves!
³ Therefore they shall be like the morning mist or dew that goes away early,
like chaff that swirls from the threshing floor or like smoke from a window.
⁴ Yet I have been the Lord your God ever since the land of Egypt;
you know no God but me, and besides me there is no savior.
⁵ It was I who fed you in the wilderness,
in the land of drought.
⁶ When I fed them, they were satisfied;
they were satisfied and their heart was proud;
therefore they forgot me.

Hosea 14:4-6

⁴ (But) I will heal their disloyalty;
I will love them freely,
For my anger has turned from them.
⁵ I will be like the dew to Israel;
He shall blossom like the lily,
He shall strike root like the forests of Lebanon.
⁶ His shoots shall spread out;
his beauty shall be like the olive tree,
And his fragrance like that of Lebanon.

(Scripture text is from *NRSV*)

47

Introduction

Have you experienced a snowfall in wintertime, or perhaps at high altitude? Have you ever experienced rainfall in the springtime? Have you ever experienced dewfall in the early dawn? But wait a minute – does the dew really fall from above?

Today we know from meteorology that dewfall is actually the condensation of water vapor from the atmosphere which takes place when the temperature of the earth's surface, and of objects near the ground, cools by the continual giving off of terrestrial radiation at nighttime. When the dewpoint is reached, condensation into liquid water begins. When the morning's sunlit warmth heats up the earth's surface and the surrounding air, the opposite phenomenon of evaporation occurs.

Today we might think of dew as a nuisance, for instance when it comes to mowing the lawn or playing a round of golf. But for the Israelites in the centuries before Christ, the appearance of the dew was a blessing representing refreshment in the hot climate. The dew was understood to be an agent of fruitfulness and was especially important in the long dry season when no rain falls. Dew-forming moisture is borne by westerly winds coming off the Mediterranean Sea.

However, in the Ancient Near East, the dew was thought to originate – just as do the snow and the rain – from a place high above the earth, from the vast storehouses of water in the heavenly realm. That is where the water was placed during the creation of the world. God created not only the material aspects of the world but was also responsible for its structure and the dynamics of its operation. Here is an example depicting dew from Proverbs 3:19–20:

> *The Lord by his wisdom founded the earth;*
> *By understanding he established the heavens;*
> *By his knowledge the deeps broke open,*
> *And the clouds drop down the dew. (NRSV)*

In the book of Job 38–40, God challenges Job to provide answers to the origins of the cosmological mysteries, in order to coax him out of his tiny sphere of understanding. Consider these questions posed, playfully and yet ironically, by God, all having to do with water and its phase changes:

> *Has the rain a father,*
> *Or who has begotten the drops of dew?*
> *From whose womb did the ice come forth,*
> *And who has given birth to the hoarfrost of heaven?*
> *The waters become hard like stone,*
> *And the face of the deep is frozen. (NRSV)*

In addition, Yahweh, Master of the Universe, was believed to make use of the elements – sunlight, rain, thunder and lightning, dew – in other words, every force of nature, to accomplish his purposes in history.

And so when the dew appeared in the cool of the morning, it was believed by the people of Israel to have arrived, as did all of the other watery types of precipitation, from heaven above. The arrival of the dew was a silent phenomenon; its coming during cool nights was almost imperceptible. It was gentle to the touch. Because of its glistening, almost diamond-like appearance on the grass and vegetation, the dew seemed to have a magical quality and was called "dew from heaven." It was one of God's silent blessings[56].

In Deuteronomy 32 we read an example of a blessing involving dew:

> *May my instruction soak in like the rain,*
> *and my discourse permeates like the dew. (NAB)*

In biblical times a spoken blessing was believed to release a power which could not be retracted, like an arrow released from a bow. By using an image taken from the realm of nature, God's instruction is compared to "the pure,

---

[56] Henry C. McCook, *The Dew: God's Silent Blessing* (1887), published by the Young Men's Christian Association, Philadelphia. This essay is Number 3 in a series called *The Gospel in Nature: A Series of Popular Discourses on Scripture Truths derived from Facts in Nature.*

gentle and insinuating influence of rain or dew."[57] And God's word, like the dew from heaven, had significance also by bridging the gap between earth and heaven. God was not only transcendent but also immanent, very close by among the people.

Join me in singing a refrain from the song "Morning Has Broken."

> *Leader intones: Like the first dewfall, on the first grass*
> *All sing: Like the first dewfall, on the first grass*

Hosea and the People's Guilt

Listen to these verses from our scripture text, Hosea 13: 1–2:

> *When Ephraim spoke, there was trembling; he was exalted in Israel;*
> *but he incurred guilt through Baal and died.*
> *² And now they keep on sinning and make a cast image for themselves,*
> *idols of silver made according to their understanding,*
> *all of them the work of artisans.*
> *"Sacrifice to these," they say. People are kissing calves! (NRSV)*

The prophet Hosea lived and preached in the northern part of the kingdom during the 8th century before Christ. Hosea is concerned with Israel's part in keeping the covenant with God. Beyond the idea of a covenant as a legal framework, there is also the inner dynamic of covenant-love.

It has been said that Hosea's favorite word is *chesed*, or covenant-love. One meaning of chesed is loving-kindness, but the Hebrew word connotes much more than this. The deeper meaning of chesed is steadfast, enduring love. If the people were to respond to God not with apathy but with unwavering loyalty to the one God and responsibility to obligations undertaken such as their covenant promise, they would be practicing chesed in response to God's covenant-love for them.

But the reality was that Israel's loyalty was divided between love of God and their attention through ritual practices to Baal, the pagan god of fertility

---

[57] *Jamieson-Fawcett-Brown Bible Commentary* (viewed online March 2013).

and storms. The people sought to manipulate Yahweh as a nature god whose only function was the provision of wine and grain. They were practicing a covert paganism and forgetting that they were God's chosen people, that God was their Maker. Other sins had crept into their lifestyles as well: they were concerned with pleasure and personal gain; they sought security in the construction of buildings and fortifications rather than relying on God for safety, and they were ungrateful. (Perhaps some of these elements are recognizable still today.) In a nutshell, the Israelites were experiencing sin-history and not salvation history!

Hosea, at one point in his preaching, proclaims that God's desire is steadfast love, not sacrifices or burnt offerings. The people were failing to practice covenant-love despite God's gifts to them throughout their history, despite the gracious mercies shown to them time and again. After all, this was the God "who brought Israel out of Egypt, and who, because of that gracious act and its accompanying covenant bond, will not fail his people, however much they fail him."[58]

Turning once again to our scripture text, we read in verse 3:

³ Therefore they shall be like the morning mist or dew that goes away early,
like chaff that swirls from the threshing floor or like smoke from a window.

All three of the images Hosea speaks about — mist or dew, chaff being stirred up and blown away, and smoke — represent things that are evanescent and dissipate rapidly. The prophet uses similes of impermanence, instability, transitoriness. The dew that goes away early fails to trickle down and provide needed moisture to the dry earth. Like the ephemeral dew, so was the love of the people of Israel for their God, according to the prophet: short-lived! Their responsive love and good conduct were too short-lived to make a positive difference, and then were gone, vanished as if into thin air. The people lacked real repentance. Moreover, if they did repent, it was shallow and not genuine, a superficial formality based in selfish concerns, and transient like the dew.

All sing: Like the first dewfall, on the first grass

---

[58] Eric C. Rust, "The Theology of Hosea," *Review and Expositor* 54, no. 4 (Fall 1957): 510–521.

Hosea and God's suffering

> *⁴ Yet I have been the Lord your God ever since the land of Egypt;*
> *you know no God but me, and besides me there is no savior.*
> *⁵ It was I who fed you in the wilderness,*
> *in the land of drought.*
> *⁶ When I fed them, they were satisfied;*
> *they were satisfied and their heart was proud;*
> *therefore they forgot me.*

God's chosen people were essentially good but had gotten in the habit of making bad choices to the extent that the whole of their lives had been corrupted. Earlier in Hosea, God in exasperation says to the people, "What shall I do with you?" One commentator has said of God's dilemma, "Goodness evanescent, that is what creates God's difficulty."[59]

God's desire for his elect, the people of Israel, was to experience salvation, or the right order of things. But they were lacking a unifying will to serve, to trust in God and to adhere to a single-minded focus on purity of heart.[60] In the time of the Ancient Near East, it was believed that the heart was the center of volition, of proper choice making, the seat of wisdom.

It may be difficult for us to imagine God being in a dilemma. But let's suppose for a moment that God was emotionally torn and was suffering over what choice to follow. Should God punish them yet again? Or love them even more, as a mother loves her child, tenderly and with perpetual care? For Hosea, Yahweh is torn with conflicting emotions: initially his righteous judgment prevails, and yet he continues to love Israel, no matter how unworthy. God is at the same time holy mystery and yet not indifferent to the people's plight.

---

[59] Donald F. Ackland, "Preaching from Hosea to a Nation in Crisis," *Southwestern Journal of Theology* 18, no. 1 (1975): 43–55.

[60] Marvin E. Tate, "The Whirlwind of a National Disaster: A Disorganized Society," *Review and Expositor* 72, no. 4 (Fall 1975): 449–463.

Hosea and God's unbounded love

In Chapter 14 of the book of Hosea we read these beautiful and comforting words:

> *⁴ I will heal their disloyalty;*
> *I will love them freely,*
> *For my anger has turned from them.*
> *⁵ I will be like the dew to Israel.*
> *He shall blossom like the lily,*
> *He shall strike root like the forests of Lebanon.*
> *⁶ His shoots shall spread out; his beauty shall be like the olive tree,*
> *And his fragrance like that of Lebanon.*

Hosea's cause for hope is the steadfastness of divine love; his theme is that God is unwearying and persistent in his enduring love for his people. God will not abandon Israel. He will love them freely, extravagantly, everlastingly, with a love that knows no bounds; and this, despite no evidence of the people turning back to God. He is ready to forgive them nonetheless. God will be faithful to his promise of chesed, of covenant-love. No longer will he call Israel "not my people" or "foolish children."

God says through the prophet, "I will be like the dew to Israel." The dew signifies divine renewal and restoration of their life, and harmony with one another and with the environment. By God's initiative and unmerited grace, the people will be loved back into wholeness. The words, "I will be like the dew" can be understood as a future rendering of "I AM."[61] God will again make their relationships secure and pour out his blessings. The people will be invigorated like the dew which comes quietly, steadily, pacifically. They will be as beautiful as the lily and as firmly rooted as the cedars in Lebanon. The dew, as a symbol of refreshment, signifies divine renewal of Israel's life and is a symbol of God's coming to bless.

"Hosea expresses poignantly Israel's longing for the divine presence, which is as assured as the annual cycle" of dewfall in the dry months.[62]

---

[61] Ronald Youngblood, "A New Occurrence of the Divine Name," *Journal of the Evangelical Theological Society* 15, no. 3 (1972): 144–152.

[62] Philip J. King, *Amos, Hosea, Micah: An Archaeological Commentary* (Louisville, KY: Westminster

Because of the coming reconciliation and blessing by God, the people will be able to bless others.

All sing: Like the first dewfall, on the first grass

Meaning for us today

What does all this 'dewfall' have to do with us today? The dew is a symbol of grace, of peace, of divine love and blessing. Despite our human frailty and constant stumbling – our 'goodness evanescent' – we are still loved by God. I once watched a film called *"Truly, Madly, Deeply."* Perhaps God's love is like the title of that film. Today for us as Christians, Jesus is a bearer of life-giving refreshment for weary souls. He is new life from heaven who entered into the realm of time and the concreteness of human experience.

The question becomes, then, am I a person who resists grace or welcomes grace? Like the ground which is softened when the dew permeates it, do I cultivate a welcoming receptivity to God's abundant, unfailing provision of grace? These words of the late Scott Peck[63] come to mind: "While we cannot will ourselves to grace, we can by will open ourselves to its miraculous coming. We can prepare ourselves to be [like] fertile ground, a welcoming place." Peck continues, "We do not come to grace; grace comes to us … we may seek it not, yet it will find us."

Abbreviations used:
NSRV – New Revised Standard Version
NAB – New American Bible

John Knox Press, 1988).
[63] M. Scott Peck, *The Road Less Traveled: A New Psychology of Love, Traditional Values and Spiritual Growth* (New York: Simon and Schuster, 1978), pp. 38 and 307.

Discussions

The discussions constitute the primary interaction with the speaker during the conference. These are monitored to insure that all questions are considered and that no one dominates the conversation. In this chapter the edited questions, comments, and responses of Professor Woloschak have been arranged alphabetically according to topic. The questions and comments of participants have often been edited for clarity. The responses by Professor Woloschak are essentially untouched.

In addition to the moonitored discussions involving all participants, there is a student only session, which is not recorded. This session takes place in the same area as the general discussions. In the discussions recorded in this chapter Professor Woloshak often referred to the student session.

There were three discussion sessions and a brief Q&A session after the Friday evening lecture. These are identified by a number 0, 1, 2, or 3 appearing in parentheses following the topic of the question or comment. The number 0 indicates the Q&A session of Friday evening (April 5, 8:30 PM), the number 1 the Saturday morning discussion (April 6, 9:00 AM), the number 2 the Saturday afternoon session (April 6, 3:30 PM), and the number 3 the Sunday morning session (April 7, 11:00 AM). The student session took place between the two Saturday sessions 1 and 2. The reader will notice that participants gain in understanding as the conference develops.

In these discussions Professor Woloschak is identified as Gayle.

In alphabetical form the topics into which the discussions were organized, with subtopics for each specific question or comment, are provided in the list below. Some topics appear in many sessions.

1. Care of Creation
Humanity and Forced Extinction
Second Coming and Care of Nature

2. Creativity
Creativity and God

8. Religion and Science

Unanswerable Questions in Science
Time in Theology and in Science
Religion and Scientific Observation
Religion and Evolution
Religion and Scientific Theory
Influence of Science on Religion (5 questions/comments)
Interwoven Biology and Theology

9. Religion

Insight from the Orthodox Tradition
Genesis and History
Grace in the Orthodox Church
Sin and Inheritance
Understanding and Temptation
Sin and Survival
Free Will Action Potential

10. Suffering

Suffering and Religion
Suffering and Free Will (2 questions/comments)
Suffering and Heaven
Suffering and Contentment
Joy in Suffering
Mentally Overcoming Suffering
Mind over Discomfort
Buddhist Tradition of Accepting
Suffering Shared in Speech
Suffering from Evolution
Suffering and Christ's Teaching
Suiffering and God's Emotions
God Suffers
A meaning in suffering
Trust and Speaking

11.Thought

Origin of Ideas

Thinking without Language (2 questions/comments)

1. Care of Creation

Humanity and Forced Extinction (1)

Question. In saying that extinction is natural do you mean to say that humanity is urged to dominate nature and in some cases that forced extinction should be deemed natural? Or are we actually changing the laws of nature?

Gayle. Thanks for that question. I should have said more about that last night, but I got sidetracked and forgot. I think if we go back and look at the extinction rates over time, the one thing that we will find about our modern era, the last 50 to 100 years, is that extinction rates are taking place at a much more rapid pace than ever before in history. And that would suggest that perhaps human intervention here is doing something that goes beyond what is natural.

Although you could argue that humans are part of nature, I am not convinced that this is a natural thing. And the net result is that we are losing diversity of life on earth, we are losing the ability to be able to have new species moving into appropriate locations.

Has anyone seen the news this week about the bees and how we are losing bees? Bees are our major pollinators for a lot of our crops. Human destruction has led to bees and all pollinators being outpaced by other insects that don't have the ability to pollinate. That is putting us at risk. We need to think hard about the rate of extinction that we have today, versus the kind of natural extinction that we have seen over many, many millions of years before us. And I am concerned about it.

I was talking to somebody last night about how Christianity was blamed for the ecological problems that exist now. In fact there was a paper in *Science* a couple years ago that said that it is Christianity's fault that we have all this killing of species going on and these extinctions. I am not sure that this thinking is part of the long-lived ancient Christian tradition. I think that what happened was the exploitation of nature. Nature was something that was co-opted by greedy industrialists who chose to use it for their purposes, and then said it was Christian. But if you look through the ancient Christian tradition, all the way back, that exploitation of nature was never part of our understanding. In fact there are saints revered by all traditions of Christianity who lived in harmony with nature, who lived with animals, who understood animals in a different sense like that story I mentioned last night where there is the guy who was feeding the poisonous snakes milk. I think that is a deep part of the Christian tradition, and I think this idea of exploiting the environment was something that was said to be Christian, but it really wasn't. So we took the blame.

Second Coming and Care of Nature (1)

Question. There is a strong Second-Coming culture at Andrews University. I imagine this is true in many Christian traditions. There is then not much motivation for stewardship of nature if God will end the whole world in fire. And Jesus will return any day. Why plan long term care for the earth when there will be no long term? Have you come across this?

Gayle. I think that is probably actually a valid point.

My own view of it is that if Jesus said that he had no idea when the end of the earth is coming, who am I to ever guess when it is going to be? So I think that is the way we have to live life. But I do agree with you that there is an upsurgance in anticipating the end of the earth.

Certainly it has been with Christianity from the very beginning. The message has always been that we should live our lives like they could end at any moment, but not that we should just exploit everything around us because of that. In fact it should be a reason for us to introvert, to think about ourselves and use that as a moment for reflection.

So I think it is a perversion of the original Christian message, which was that Christ's coming is a reason to be better persons, not a reason to exploit everything around you because the world is going to blow up anyway, so who cares.

This is also an argument that people use for capital punishment. They say, look, God is going to take care of it in the end anyway, so who cares if we kill them. There's a second world after this, so it is meaningless.

I think that those sorts of arguments keep us from making proper judgment and proper discernment here. Those are the things we should never be putting off, those are the things we should be dealing with every moment. But I do agree, I think that is a reason why it comes up often.

Comment. The topic of the end of the world comes up in Paul's letters to the Thessalonians. Paul was writing to people who thought that humanity was going to be wiped out in the next generation, were ceasing to do the right thing, and were failing to make the right choices in their lives. That didn't happen for them. But it does have a scriptural history or memory, and so Paul was really preaching that people need to be upright, be Christians, and get out of that mindset.

[2 Thessalonians 1-3: *To turn now, brothers, to the coming of our Lord Jesus Christ and how we shall all be gathered round him: please do not get excited too soon or alarmed by any prediction or rumor or any letter claiming to come from us, implying that the day of the Lord has already arrived. Never let anyone deceive you in this way.*
2 Thessalonians 13-15: *But we feel that we must be continually be thanking God for you, brothers whom the Lord loves, because God chose you from the beginning to be saved by the sanctifying Spirit and by faith in the truth. Through the good news that we brought he called you to this so that you should share in the glory of our Lord Jesus Christ. Stand firm then, brothers, and keep the traditions that we taught you, whether by word of mouth or by letter.*]

Comment. Just briefly, in the same spirit, and speaking from the Adventist tradition as well, I am going to affirm the point that you made. We ought to understand that the imminence of Christ's coming is a reason and a motivation to be found faithful in our perseverance while we wait. If he comes and we are not faithful in our Christian life then he comes as our judge.

Comment. In Romans Paul talks about how the Christians are storing up wrath for themselves in the coming judgment. So there is a dual consequence to the eschaton. There is either God's peace or there is God's wrath. We reach God's wrath if we do bad things. But we reach God's peace by doing good works. What we do does matter.

The lion will lie down with the lamb. There will be a New Jerusalem. God is Judge. We cannot judge.

2. Creativity

Hypotheses and Creativity (1)

Comment. Charles Sanders Peirce,[64] a logician who formulated the hypothetical deductive principle, considered creativity very important. And then of course you have Whitehead for whom creativity was a first principle. I don't think the principle of Whiteheadian creativity is explored the way it ought to be.

Gayle. There is another part that also comes in, I think, when there is hypothesis testing going on. Sometimes the results take you in a direction that you didn't at all predict from your hypothesis. This happens particularly in biology a lot, because biology is just very complicated. It takes creativity to see that something is important and you should follow it, even though it is not really what you originally hypothesized. You are doing the experiments to test an hypothesis, but the experiments didn't come out to be what you wanted. And it is very hard to discern whether that is because of something that is important and you should follow it, or if it is an artifact that you can spend five years explaining, but is meaningless. Particularly for grad students, who want to get done with their thesis, that is very important.

Creativity and God (1)

Comment. Last evening you mentioned the different ways of knowing through the arts, music and so on. I think that is also true of theology. And creativity in the sciences is essential. The most creative minds are pushing back the frontiers. I heard a theologian once say that creative love is what God is about. Maybe it's part of what makes us human.

Gayle: I will agree with you that creativity is one of the things that make us human. I am going to go back to Bulgakov; you are going to be sick of him by the end of this. But Bulgakov said something about God as Creator and

---

[64] Charles Sanders Peirce was an American philosopher, logician, and scientist, sometimes known as the father of pragmatism.

humans as being creators with a small "c." And I know that I will probably get some people upset with this, but I will say it anyway.

He was strongly against the Augustinian idea of calling God a cause, because cause is something about which you can actually say, "I sat down and caused this to happen." For example I can say that I'm going to write this paper and I cause it to happen, since it comes out of my mind. But creativity is something that you can't actually do on demand. You can't say, "Oh, I'm going to set aside this hour as that during which to be creative today." It doesn't happen that way. And yet creativity, I think, imbues every part of human existence. By this I mean all of those things that come from creativity, including artistic expression (I used that quote from Ayala[65]). It's something special about humanity. And Bulgakov saw it as a way in which we are all sort of God like. He considered it wrong to call God a cause, but rather to always call him Creator, because Creator is the more accurate way to describe it. That harkens back to our own human creativity. So I do agree, I think that is something special about humans. When, though, did humans evolve that ability to be creative? That is a much harder question.

Creativity and Evolution (1)

Question. I have been struggling with this question for a number of years, since reading Richard Dawkins's *The Selfish Gene*, in which he tried, somewhat unsuccessfully, to argue that acts of altruism can all be explained by evolution. If we accept that evolution, which depends on competition, is God's ultimate creativity, how do we then come to a system of ethics as human beings that takes us beyond that principle of evolution? Is that where some of the stories of Genesis begin to teach us about the ways of God versus the way of God's creation?

Gayle. I thought a little bit about that issue. So let me do my best to explain it.

I don't think that the competition should be viewed so much as a path to deciding which one is better. It deals with utilitarian purposes. One could

---

[65] Francisco Ayala is a Spanish-American evolutionary biologist and philosopher at the University of California, Irvine. He was ordained a Dominican priest in 1960, but left the priesthood that same year.

argue that in societies, or in churches, or in a broad sense, you try to choose the person that best does that job to be the leader of the community. For example, consider that you try to choose the person to lead the choir. That is an issue of choice. The difference in evolution is that the choice appears to be random. The mutation that occurs is random. That is the part where it becomes hard.

Say we are going to randomly pick a choir director. You would never randomly pick a choir director. Well, maybe you would. But you would really be in trouble. What we can say, however, is that it may appear that the people you have to choose from have been selected at random. And the one that is best suited is the one you pick. That issue of randomness is one that Sir Arthur Peacock tried to deal with directly.

I don't know how many of you know the story of Arthur Peacocke.[66] He was an Anglican priest. He was one of the best leaders in the scientific community. He was a brilliant scientist. He got worried about the evolution issue and said, "Oh, my, this is going to make everybody lose their faith because there is randomness. I am going to change and become a theologian." He became a world-class theologian and has written about fifty books. He died a couple years ago. I actually met his wife.

What Arthur Peacock did was he tried to look at that randomness issue, and asked, "Why would this make people not believe in God?"

In my way of thinking about it, whether we know it or not, we need randomness to survive. In our own bodies, how do we fight an infection? How could it ever be that your body can be tuned to fight every infection it might ever encounter in all its life? And you know what? The person next to you can encounter every infection they would ever find during their lives, and they're never going to be the same set of infections, right? It's because our immune system has randomness built into it that allows our bodies to function in that way. So there is some way in which we need randomness to survive. And that is where the evolution comes in.

The randomness allows for the generation of mutations. But it is the natural environment that allows us to be able to select for what is best suited.

---

[66] Arthur Peacocke (1924-2006) was an English biochemist and Episcopal Priest. His landmark book on theology and science was *Theology for a Scientific Age*.

And that is how that relationship works best. I don't know if that answers your question, it's sort of my thinking about it.

3. Evolution
Evolution and Eugenics (1)

Question. You made it clear last night that survival of the fittest is a method for biological processes, but that it is not necessarily so for other domains. How would you explain or give examples to fearful Christians about that? Particularly, I've had conversations about why eugenics is not necessarily the right answer if evolution is true. Could you comment on that, please?

Gayle. That is a very important issue. One of the reasons that I think people discard evolution is because they say, "Well, survival of the fittest makes the world appear mean. We should have eugenics and we should just go ahead and select ourselves for what's best." Well the thing about eugenics is that nature is not selecting. There, human beings are selecting, and whom we select for might not be what nature would select for.

Realize that nature is an unbiased selector because it is actually just about what survives. But it is biased because the things that are best for that environment are what survive. Now what is best for that environment may not be what is best for any other environment.

What do we say about malaria and sickle cell anemia? In Africa there is an advantage for humans to have both one copy of the sickle cell gene and one copy of the normal gene for hemoglobin. But in America there is no selection for it. So if natural evolution took place and we had no interventions for sickle cell anemia, everybody that had the one abnormal gene would eventually die out of the population by natural selection. If eugenics operated, then we might actually engineer out the gene for sickle cell, even in Africa, not knowing better, and create a population that could not survive in that environment because we have no clue why a lot of these mutations developed in the first place. Sickle cell is one I can point to and tell you there was an advantage. But there are probably a million others for which we have no clue why there was even a selection to have those mutations in the human population. We don't understand. How dare we think that we can actually choose?

Maybe a worse situation is selection that is going on in the womb right now. There are actually agencies that will allow for choices of the attributes of a baby. We have *in vitro* fertilization taking place. There are agencies that allow you to design your baby. For example you say, "I want blue eyes," checked, "I want male," checked, "I want brown hair," checked, and we promise that we give you 90% odds of this kind of baby. You can find the websites. In California there are about ten of these. And there are a lot on the Internet that do this. They do genetic selection. So what they do is they pick the egg that is going to give those particular features, they take the sperm that is going to give those particular features, then they do the *in vitro* fertilization, and here you go, you have the baby you wanted. And that is the form of eugenics in actual fact. But here the parents are selecting what they want for their baby. I personally think it is a dangerous thing.

I should finish it up by saying that I worry not just about its being used in eugenics situations. I also worry when people start talking about cultures. We start saying, "Ah, it's the survival of the fittest culture." And, therefore, when the Indian nation loses their language and they are wiped off the face of the earth, well, it is the survival of the fittest. And it was obviously the European culture that was the best. That is what survived here in the US.

That is absolutely ridiculous. The principle of survival of the fittest has been shown to occur in biological systems but not in culture, not in language, not in anything else. You can't take the principles of physics and apply them necessarily to biology. For instance you can't say that because there is a gravitational force in physics that there is a similar force that drives cells to bind together. And you can't do the same thing from biology to social sciences. You can't claim that survival of the fittest is what happens culturally, or with languages, or anything else. But I have heard people do that. There are some people who do believe that there is an inheritance of things called memes, which are cultural units that are much like genes. But there is no evidence that cultural traits work by a survival of the fittest mechanism.

Evolution and Cooperation (1)

Comment. As an ecologist I think that one thing that our field is guilty of in the last decade is overemphasizing competition in terms of evolutionary theory. More recently there has been a renewed emphasis on cooperation. Mutualisms are ubiquitous. Microbes are in our gut. Creative processes are built probably even more on cooperative interactions than on competitive ones. And that I think will help us perhaps in the future reframe that topic.

Gayle. Yes, thanks so much for that, you are absolutely correct. Absolutely!

4. Genes
Regulation of Genes (0)

Question: Early in your lecture you said that human genes are expressed at higher levels. Is there an answer for that at a scientific level?

Gayle. That's a really good question. There are gene regulations, particularly in humans. Let me put it in context. Human beings have 40,000 genes. The fruit fly has about 50 or 60,000 genes. So, you look at the fruit fly and you ask why fruit flies have 50,000 genes and we have only 40,000 genes? Well, it is because humans have a very, very complicated way of turning on and off genes.

I have a student who studied one region that controls a gene. She used a different color for each control region. On the computer, which handled approximately 120 colors, she did four different runs of this and still ran out of colors. That's how complicated it is.

Probably between the chimpanzee and the human, what happened was that certain control regions became much more efficient in humans than they were in the chimp. And that is what has allowed them to reach a very, very high level in humans, and not quite reach it in the chimpanzee. That doesn't mean that the sequences are different. It just means that they are more efficient in humans.

There is also a difference in timing for some of them. There are some genes that get turned on in day six of development in humans, and they get turned on in day eight of the chimpanzee, particularly for things that involve brain development. So probably that timing is also very important.

Question (continued). Is there any particular reason that would be the case?

Gayle. It was not what was predicted. Certainly having higher levels of controls for the majority of them was not at all predicted. It could have been lower for some genes. There could have been some that never got turned on at all. So, it's a mystery, still. That's the good thing about science; it asks more questions than it answers.

Systems Approach (0)

Comment. You pointed out that within an organism there are higher levels and lower levels of interaction. For example the brain influences the genes while the genes have influenced the development of the brain. And then there is the influence of the environment during evolution. Organisms interact with one another. You seem to be implying that there should be a new methodology for science, which moves away from pure analysis to synthesis.

Gayle. Thanks so much for that comment.

Many of us talk about this among ourselves. I think that what has happened, particularly in biology, but I would say in most of science, is that everything becomes very, very focused. I know people who specialize in one particular sequence of one part of a gene. And that is what they spend their entire careers studying. They might try to put it in context a little bit, but it is that one little pathway that they are involved in. When we start to put things together, they become so complicated that only my computer can understand it. I can't. But that it seems complicated is also a worry, because we are not trying to understand a big picture. You don't get grant money to study a big picture. You get grant money to study little parts.

Now there are some people that are trying to put things together. There are systems biology people that are trying to put it together using computational approaches. But I think that scientists themselves need to be broader in their way of thinking about things. So I think you are exactly right on that. I hope that thinking out-of-the-box in a broader sense will help to some extent. I have noticed that as we get more and more gray hairs, we do tend to think in broader terms. So I am hoping that as the scientific group ages, that will happen. But if we are not putting up young people to join in, then there could be problems.

5. Human Distinction

Human Distinction (1)

Question. I am an ecologist from Goshen College. One of the questions you raised last night, and one of the probing questions that we might give attention to in the future, is the question of when we became human. I would like you to comment on that. Do you think it is an answerable question? And if it is, why is it important? What are some of the reasons you think it is important?

Gayle. I am not sure it is answerable. The reason I think it might be important is because it might tell us which features we consider to be unique in humans, and what makes us somehow separate from everything else that did exist and that does exist.

I think it is easier to answer the question of how we compare to other species alive now. This question becomes very difficult to answer when we try to go back in our evolutionary history and ask at what point this occured. We are now the only *Homo* species that exists on earth. But there were times when multiple *Homo* species were living on earth simultaneously. Or at least that is what the hypothesis says. And that is the answer many of the archaeologists and physical anthropologists would give. What made *Homo sapiens* distinct from those other *Homo* species, like *Homo erectus* and others? I think that might tell us something about who human beings are.

Is it an answerable question? I am not sure because I have this feeling that who we are has much more to do with who we are culturally, how we interact, how we communicate, and how we live our lives. And that is something that is not so easy to discern from the archaeological record. So we might be able to get the gene sequence of the *Homo erectus*, or the Neanderthal, which appears to have been *Homo* as well, and be able to compare it and say, "Whoa, there are some Neanderthal genes in *Homo sapiens*." But in the end that doesn't tell us that much about culture, what life was like, and things like that.

We can look at genes that we know are associated with cognition or that are associated with particular behavioral changes, and see how frequent they were in the Neanderthal populations. But we don't have enough of a record to be able to answer that yet. And I don't know that it is ever going to be answerable. But I think it is one of those things that we would love to find, because it might help us, tell us why we think humans are different.

Relationship to God (2)

Question. Did God have a relationship with homonins, those early humans? Does it matter? And then is there a threshold of intelligence that is necessary to have that relationship with God? If so, how does that reflect on deficient intelligence among humans?

Gayle. Let me say that my dog has a relationship with God. So I think all creatures, all of life does. That issue about intelligence is a really important one. I am going to talk about it from the Orthodox perspective. I obviously know my own tradition well, and I can talk about that. I can't always talk about everybody else's tradition. But I will talk about the Orthodox tradition with regard to intelligence.

Orthodox are unusual among Christians because we baptize, chrismate [christen] and give Holy Communion all on the same day. So the day I was baptized, when I was two months old, I was chrismated and I received Holy Communion.

And our teaching asks, in essense, who are you to say that there is a certain intelligence that's required to understand what you received. When I receive communion do I understand it in its mystery and its depth? No. Who is to say that the two month old doesn't understand it better than I do? And so we do give communion to people who are mentally disabled in whatever form, because they are members of the church just like the two month old, or the one month old. They are seen as being equal. The depth of understanding here relative to an understanding of God is almost meaningless.

Having said that I don't think I can answer the question about early pre-humans, because I just don't think we know enough about what their relationship might be. I mean one could argue that they were on a journey, too. I just don't know.

Relationship to God (2)

Question. Would it have mattered if they did have some kind of relationship with God and then God let them become extinct? Would that matter to you theologically? Biologically?

Gayle. I don't think that would matter at all. If we keep going on in environmental problems like we are, we may dead-end too. And I don't think we know what our biological future is. I don't think our relationship with God is dependent on humanity continuing to exist in its current form forever.

Special Place of Humans (2)

Question. But don't you consider that there is really something unique about humans? And should we not realize that this places us in a special location in the order of things?

Gayle. You are asking me whether I think that human beings are special. You know, that's really a hard question. Let me do my best. But I can punch holes through this thinking, too.

Thinking human beings are special has gotten us into trouble because then we consider ourselves to be something unique in creation. Therefore nothing else is important. So who cares if we go and eat up the forests and destroy everything?

That said, I do think that there are things that are special about human beings. We are the portion of creation that contemplates. We are the portion of creation that thinks beyond ourselves. And because of that I think there is a great responsibility on our shoulders. So that specialness is not so much that we think we are so great and wonderful. It's that more is expected of us because of that. And the expectation is being responsible for each other, being responsible for our planet, being responsible for the cosmos. And that is a burden that makes us special. It is not because we are so cool and so great.

As I said to the students earlier, and probably most people in this room would not like to hear this, my dog is a better dog than I am a human being. My dog doesn't need to be taught how to be a good dog. But I needed to be taught how to be a good human being. And I think that says something about our place in creation.

Proper Use of Technology (2)

Question. This morning you said something I think is very valid about technology. You are correct in saying that we often assume that technology will solve all of our problems. But that is really worrisome in many respects. It is inevitable that technology is going to be part of any solution. We can't, however, just assume that we are going to have a techno-fix for the problems. There are lots of grays. How do we begin to navigate our inevitable dependence on technology? And how do we try to figure out just how complicated and nuanced our relationship with technology is?

Gayle. Let me just say a couple things first in a broad sense, and then I'll give a couple of examples.

Obviously I've got an iPhone in my pocket, and I've got an iPad in my bag and you see me using a computer. So you know, I'm techno-maniac to some extent. I love technology and I use it a lot, and I do believe that humanity's ability to use technology is a gift. I actually see this ability as a gift from God. But that means we have the ability to use it for good or for bad.

Most often the choice isn't between whether we are going to use this for only good purposes or only bad purposes. I think the biggest issue is how we are going to be responsible for the technology.

I work in a radiation field, I do work with nuclear power, nuclear reactors, and I've been to Chernobyl, and I've been to Fukushima. And what I can tell you is that nuclear power is something that I believe in. It is a relatively clean power source for the world. But with the use of nuclear power comes a great responsibility to take care of it, and to use that power properly.

The situation in Chernobyl was very different from the situation in Fukushima. In Chernobyl it was a totally failed design of the nuclear power plant. This was known to be a failed power plant design, and it was used. It was a power plant that was both making plutonium for weapons and producing energy. And that design had been turned down by many other places in the world. But it was used there. In my opinion it should not have been used at all! That was why the reactor failed. Then we pay the price for it. The US had one reactor like that up in Hanford, Washington, and we actually shut down the reactor, but only after Chernobyl. We didn't shut it down before Chernobyl even though it was known that they were flawed designs.

The Fukushima situation I see as the opposite. In my opinion there they had a reactor that was very strong. They had a good case for needing nuclear power. A natural disaster happened. The reactor actually withstood the natural disaster very well. But then when the tsunami came it was just too much. And the reactor finally broke down.

In both cases we had sort of similar traumatic events. But in Japan they actually handled it. Despite everything you read here in the media, they handled it pretty well. They contained it. They got their people out of there. They evacuated. They reported it to the world. And they called in international help. In Chernobyl the Soviet Union did not tell anyone about it for three days. It was discovered because the reindeer farmers, the guys who herd reindeer for food up in Lapland,[67] discovered they had no more lichen for their reindeer to eat, and so they had to then move to new places. Lichen are very sensitive to radiation, and so they had a problem.

Nothing would have stopped Fukushima from happening. But at least what happened was well controlled. Chernobyl blew all over the place, sent radiation all over Eastern Europe and through much of Scandinavia as well. And it not only should it never have happened, but it was not handled responsibly after it happened. And so I think that that sort of level of responsibility is where much of how we handle technology has to come in. How can we handle it so that we prevent having accidents as much as possible, but can be prepared so that when they do happen we can keep them controlled? That is, I think, the biggest issue. And unfortunately all of that costs money. And we often use the technology without putting in place the money that is needed to make it be safe.

Limiting Technology and being more Human (3)

Question. Human creativity drives technology. But I am concerned about what choices to make in our fast-paced world that technology makes possible, at least for people who have access to it. I have a computer at home but have elected to have no Internet. That sometimes causes problems when I try to install software. I have to make numerous phone calls to get the right code numbers to do something on my desktop computer. Nevertheless I do not

---

[67] Lapland is in the northern part of Sweden and Finland.

want to get sucked into some technology just because others are. But that might be a bad attitude. Can you comment on this?

Gayle. I agree with you. In my opinion regulation of technology has to be accomplished with every person. I don't think there is going to be a broad regulation of technology that is ever going to come from anything within science, within government, or within anything else. Ultimately everything becomes personal regulation. So you have to make your own choices, as you have done, saying I'm not going to have Internet at home. Those are hard decisions.

I'm Eastern Orthodox. It's my Lent right now. We didn't have Easter yet. We will have it a few weeks from now. And a lot of people choose, during Lent, to say, I'm going to cut back on my Internet usage. I'm going to cut back on my computer time. I'm going to cut back on my TV use. Because they know that those are weaknesses for them. And spending an extra hour of the day even just talking with somebody might be healthier for them than to spend it sitting at a computer or playing a computer game.

I'll use my own example. I love music. I went off rock music one Lent. I didn't listen to any rock music on my iPad, my iPod, in my car or anywhere. And it was really hard because I was driving back and forth to work an hour and a half each day each way. And, boy, I learned a lot. I went off rock music. And you know what? I didn't get so irritated when I was driving the car. I didn't get so mad at the other drivers.

So you learn something from that experience, from going off it, from not having it available to you. And while it is a hardship, there is no question that stepping away is really important. Particularly in this age of technology we need to think hard about what we are doing, what we are doing with our time, what we are doing with our situations.

I emailed with my brother every week, but when was the last time we talked over the phone? So I pick up the phone and talk to him every other week. It is then not just an email conversation. And that is a whole different situation. You get a whole different feeling for things.

So I think that everybody needs to examine, in their own personal life, where the weaknesses are, and some times just go off it for a little while and see what happens. I learned stuff I just didn't expect from the rock music story. I never would have predicted that would happen. So that's the only thing I can say.

6. Natural Law

Evolving laws of Science (0)

Question. I agree that there is considerable evidence for evolution. And then you said that natural laws evolve and used the example that we think things started with RNA. But that doesn't match the central dogma of DNA to RNA to protein. Of course we also know that the central dogma doesn't work for many parts of our genome. There are many RNAs that don't make protein. How do you see the use of natural laws?

Gayle. This is a process that has been evolving in my brain for a while. So I will do my best to talk you through it, but I can't promise that it is fully developed.

Don York[68] is a physicist at the University of Chicago who gives a talk in the Epic of Creation course, which I teach in the Zygon Center. And every year he comes in and he tells me, "Gayle, the laws of physics changed. They were one thing at the Big Bang, and those laws were different a moment after, and they are another thing today than they were then. The laws of physics changed."

And I believe that in some sense that has to be true for biology as well. The earliest form of life was not DNA-based. Now it is true that there are organisms that do have our RNA, right now. And they still always go through a DNA intermediate in most cases. But in the RNA world that people talk about, and even this is speculative, the RNA was serving as the genetic material without any DNA dependence. That is against our dogmas today and how we think about things. It is against the way in which all of life works on earth right now. Therefore that's a law that seems to be different now.

I believe that there are some more things in chemistry that chemists have told me may be different between the chemistry laws in the early mix of the earth versus now, but I can't name those specifically because I am not a chemist.

---

[68] Donald G. York is Horace B. Horton Professor Emeritus, Department of Astronomy and Astrophysics, University of Chicago.

So that's sort of my way of thinking about it. I can't say that I can give you fifty examples. This idea is still evolving in my mind. But I actually think it is important. Because if the laws do change, if they do evolve with time, that means that they are not so static. And if we think about a God who transcends time, then we have to think a little bit about what those laws mean to God, too. I am not sure that the laws exist to God in that same sense. They may have been put there for us. But they probably don't exist in that same sense to God. So you caught me in the middle of thoughts.

Natural Law in Science and Philosophy (0)

Question. You began with a joke regarding whether we are talking the same language or a different language. I wonder if theology and philosophy simply have such a fundamentally different concept of what natural law is that, even if there are changes in the laws of physics and the laws of biology, what philosophy and theology mean by natural law is so fundamentally different that we are comparing apples to oranges.

Likewise, considering what it means to be normal, to talk about normality, is to claim one use of the word normal. It's only descriptive. In ethics, theology, and philosophy, however, what is meant by normality is really a normative claim. Again it's kind of an apples and oranges, and we end up inadvertently talking past one another.

Gayle. I think that is probably very true. Often when we join in a conversation we are talking at cross purposes. We understand things in different perspectives. And it might be that what I am saying speaks more to the scientist than it does to the philosopher or the theologian. But I do think in our culture there are certain kinds of things that I read in the newspaper that somehow speak to the non-academic person who is reading them.

So when I talk to my ninety-year-old father about normal and abnormal, I think that he understands that more in a scientific sense than a philosophical sense. So that there needs to be some sort of blunting of that discussion, or deepening of that thinking, is the main point that I am trying to make.

And that is the beauty of it too, though. To some extent that we can all get together in a room like this and come from diverse backgrounds and still try to communicate, that I think is a very beautiful thing.

Changes in Natural Law (0)

Question. One of the definite impacts of philosophy and theology on early modern science was to consider natural law as part of a clockwork universe. Therefore the natural laws would never change, because they are used indirectly as a proof for the existence of God and the stability of nature. It was all but heresy to question the universality of natural law. And now I think it is time for philosophy and theology to learn from science, especially the sciences that are based more on statistical probabilities than universal principles. Maybe philosophers and theologians should start rethinking about what they mean by about natural law and what that would imply for God as actually being a little more creative and dynamic than we customarily give God credit for.

Gayle. Yes, I think that is a good thought. I will make one comment, though. I don't believe that natural laws are changing with great frequency. I mean, I am talking in terms of beyond billions of years. At the origin of the universe, which most people believe was 13.8 billion years ago, the laws of nature were different than they are today. Maybe they changed a few times in between. But the point is that maybe on other solar systems in other galaxies in a dark star, it may be very different. That is what my physicist friends tell me. And that makes us have to think that what we see may not always be. Things may not be static in a long-term perspective.

Natural Law In Science and theology (1)

Question. I think natural law is a concept that has two different meanings. Historically, in my own discipline of philosophy and theology, the meaning of natural law has changed dramatically several times. Would you reflect, from a scientist's point of view, on what you understand theologians to be talking about when we speak of natural law?

Gayle. When scientists are talking about natural law they are talking about the laws of nature and the things that would appear to be unchangeable over time. What we were taught, as scientists, is that we are trying to understand the things that do not change over time. We are trying to come up with actual laws that do not change. I think natural law, from a more philosophical approach, deals with things that we understand and that occur in nature, but have broader applications other than just scientific principles.

So I think there is a distinction between what we are talking about from a scientific perspective versus a more philosophical perspective. The two are closely related. I think your point is exactly right. In one case we are describing nature in a very, very precise way, which is what we are trying to do scientifically. Whereas in the other case we are trying to understand what goes on in nature and sort of apply it in a broad sense to what happens in humanity and in the world.

The thing I see changing among scientists is this idea that laws of nature are absolutely permanent and always occur. What I think I am seeing now among scientists is, at least over a broad, broad perspective of billions of years, that people are willing to say that the laws of nature we describe today may not have been the laws of nature that occurred billions and billions of years ago. And I think that is a major change in the way we think about things, because that sense of permanence is no longer there in the same way.

That does not mean that if we look at nature today and look at it tomorrow they will look differently. But I think that there may be more flexibility in systems than we had before. I think that is a very important component. Maybe you should expand upon that thought. I would like to hear it from a more philosophical perspective as well.

Question (continued). My early training especially in philosophical ethics was very historical. So when we first started talking about natural law, we were looking at the Stoics from whom the Christian tradition develops a good deal of its ethical framework. Particularly the Roman version of stoicism considered the fact that the Empire had such great diversity that there were laws that were local, and they honored that by and large. But there was a common domain of human behavior that determined what was acceptable and what was unacceptable. And that became known as natural law. So even the Roman law considered this understanding of natural law to be a limitation. There was a common body of material, determining appropriate or inappropriate behavior, within which they tried to operate with diversity.

But in later times we assumed that there was a fundamental set of first principles, like mathematical underlying principles in this physical world that would underlie human behavior and human nature. And I think that is where, in our tradition, the solidification of the unchangeability of what it was to be a person or to be a human society then became normative. And this has become, in much of our moral theology, normative in terms of what is acceptable or unacceptable, natural or unnatural. There are a lot of connotations that get a little shaky, I think, when we apply them out on the fringe areas of life.

Gayle. The other thing that is worth thinking about is that there is a distinction, I think, among scientists between sort of the hard sciences and the soft sciences. But I don't know. Congress is saying now that political science is no longer a science. But how can we apply that idea of the laws of nature suddenly to say psychology? Can we say that this is predictive, this always happens? That becomes sort of the division between the hard and soft sciences. How easy is it to draw conclusions on nature based on what you can observe?

Changes in the Laws of Physics (1)

Question. You said last night that your physicist friend claimed that the laws of physics have changed since the Big Bang about 13.8 billion years ago. Are you referring to the difference in the laws of physics in the Planck Time (10^{-43} seconds) and then later after the forces separated from a unified form? I think some people had the impression that you claimed the laws changed over periods of billions of years.

Gayle. Let me try to clarify a bit. I have to be honest. I am not a physicist. So I put in all the caveats and I am only interpreting what Don York has been teaching our Zygon students for a number of years. And it is during that Big Bang moment that he is talking about for one thing. But he also says that probably elsewhere in the universe there are places where the laws of physics are different than they are here. For instance in situations in dark matter, and other areas of the universe, there could be places where the laws of physics are different. He gave some examples, but I can't remember exactly what they are. I am sorry. I am not a physicist. Maybe somebody else who is a physicist can help me on that.

Question (continued). The question is whether we actually have any data to support that, or whether it is just a supposition.

Gayle. Well he actually has data. I mean, he is an astrophysicist and he deals with things that happened within the first few moments of the Big Bang, and beyond that. And he has some data that he says indicate that there are certain things that could not have happened if the laws of physics were the same way they are now. So he has data to support that. But I don't think he is the only one. I mean we have had three other physicists that have come in to lecture, that are all astrophysicists, and they have all said exactly the same thing.

Thomist Philosophy and Modern Science (1)

Comment. I am a Jesuit, and I was educated through seven years of Thomistic philosophy and theology which I revere as a mental masterpiece for its day. But it is clearly derived from Aristotelian logic, with the major-minor conclusions of a way of thinking. And what I saw coming into being with the era of early modern science and then moving forward, getting more conscious of itself, is what I call scientific method, which is hypothesis verification. Now that got a big boost with Kant, because he was saying basically, we construct the structures and then in our minds, after having looked at our data, we try to verify them.

I honestly think that has great value for the religion and science discussion, if you stick to the scientific method. Because then what you are really saying is that the laws of nature, insofar as they came forward from God's mind, are still out there and we are dealing with nothing more than approximations to those laws.

Now some of them are pretty darn good, and very, very consistent. But we really don't know what nature is capable of in the fullest sense. The example that I give the students in class is, if you were in the early modern period[69] and told people that they would someday be able to step into a machine that was much heavier than air and eventually fly at 500 mph, they would have locked you up. You are totally out of your mind. But it was there, waiting for, first of all, someone to build a machine that would travel fast

---

[69] In philosophy the modern period begins with the introduction of the mechanistic description of nature (Newtonian Mechanics) in 1687.

enough on the ground, and then the principles of aerodynamics to get the lift, and it is perfectly natural right now.

Gayle. I would like to comment. I agree with you. I think your points are well made. I need to make sure I clarify this issue, however, because there is a lot of discussion within the scientific community, in a broad sense, regarding hypothesis driven research. There is a misunderstanding that this is the only way in which science operates: you have an hypothesis and you go to test it. But the fact of the matter is that there is probably a step that involves a great deal of creativity that comes before you actually have the hypothesis in the first place. So there is a creative component to it that gets lost in that hypothesis-driven work.

And for me, working with students, I find that it is very important to try to teach them not to suppress that creativity because of the hypothesis. Often the hypothesis is so limiting, that you don't think outside of the box at all, and you are trapped by your hypothesis, you can't go any farther.

Today's science is not just hypothesis driven. At breakfast some of us were talking about the human genome project. The human genome project was not hypothesis driven research. It was a "let's go out and sequence everything that we can find and see what we can do with it." The questions that came from it were hypothesis driven. I have the hypothesis that this gene mutated in this particular disease. And then you go and test that hypothesis by looking at the sequence. But the hypothesis was not tested by the experiment anymore, it was tested by the computer when you went and looked at it.

So there has been sort of this change in the way we think about science, because there is both the hypothesis driven and the sort of broad approach, where the hypothesis comes long after all the science has been done, sometimes years, maybe even decades later. So I think that is a distinction that needs to be made. And it probably applies to many other disciplines as well. Particularly that creative component, I think you can find that in every discipline, and no scientist in the room wants to disagree with me, so I guess that is good.

Natural Law and Freedom (2)

Question. I have been thinking about the relationship between freedom and determinism in these dialogues between science and theology. Recently, in another dialogue between science and theology, a fellow theologian said we have to choose either the deterministic world view, or a worldview of freedom, but we can't bridge the two. Would you have any thoughts or comments about that?

Gayle. That is a hard one, but let me do my best.

I'm not really a determinist. I do believe in a free creation. And I believe that we have freedom in what we choose to do. What I would say is, though, that somehow then we have to explain how an all-knowing God functions in a world that has freedom. The way I think of it, and this is my own mental view, has to do with the concept of time that I was talking about earlier. If time is irrelevant to God, and God knows, as I told the students, that each of us will be sitting in this room today at exactly this time, which I believe is true, and knew that at the beginning of creation and knows it at every moment, it doesn't mean necessarily that it was determined that this would happen.

So we have a freedom that brought us here. But God knew that would happen. God is a mystery. I tend to understand God using words like uncreated, unintelligible, all those un-words. And I don't think I can understand God better than that. I'm not sure that I can even put my mind around it. I think that the general concept of freedom, in the context of an all-knowing God is the best way that I can explain it. I know they are a bit contradictory.

Question (continued). Can you relate this to the question of natural law? As I understand it, human beings operate in a world of natural law. Yet we are able to operate freely in that world, within limits. Natural laws limit, but do not require us to do what we do freely.

How do you conceptualize God's activity in the world? Do the natural laws, as understood by science, leave room for God to interact with the world? Or does God just start everything off at the beginning, and never can interact anymore because the natural laws keep God out. If we are free to act within this natural law framework, why not God?

Gayle. I said this to the students, but let me explain it from a concept of prayer.

I believe that when I pray for something, or if anyone prays for something, in a sense that is a cosmic prayer. God heard that prayer a gazillion years ago. Before I was ever around God heard that prayer. In a way it becomes a part of the cosmos. And in that joining in a cosmic prayer, God knew I was going to pray it. And things happen the way they did knowing that God was going to hear that prayer.

I don't ever want to say that moment by moment God is sticking a finger in. But God has absolute freedom to do anything. If God so chooses let nature be overcome. So I think that in that concept, that we must allow for total freedom. But it seems to me that it is a cosmic perspective, not an in-time perspective as we feel it.

Paradox of Zeno (2)

Comment. In my history of mathematics course I often discuss the paradoxes of Zeno of Elea. Most of them can now be settled thanks to differential and integral calculus. But there is one that stands out, that I think it is becoming very important. It is the flying arrow. Zeno claims that the arrow is fixed all the time. We are under the impression that it moves, but it really is a succession of non-movements. Motion is an illusion, according to Zeno. Perhaps, stretching the analogy, natural reality is just as mysterious as what we studied in theology. We are in mystery wall to wall.

Gayle. And let me just add that, even in biology, a lot of the conclusions we draw are actually just inference. We aren't really seeing what we think we are seeing. We develop an assay to monitor what we think. If that assay is flawed, then the results are flawed, and we are not really seeing what we think we are seeing. For instance we never see a gene turn on. We see the result of the gene turning on. We see a change in a gene structure that tells us it turns on. But we never see it actually turn on. So I think that we do draw a lot of inferences about things that we may find are not actually reality at some point in time. So it's very interesting. And then of course there is Heisenberg's uncertainty principle where, just the action of measuring something changes it anyway, so there we go.

7. Normalcy

Normal and Abnormal (0)

Question. You raised the question of what is normal. Is it possible to ask, or begin to answer, what is abnormal? If only one person has a particular gene mutation, which causes some problem for that individual, that could be abnormal. And how would you know if it is? Maybe there is some evolutionary benefit on the way.

Gayle. Yes, I think that's a good point. I think we have to get totally away from this thinking of normal and abnormal. And we may have to get away from even calling something abnormal. We may have to call many things polymorphisms that we previously called mutations.

Many polymorphisms have effects that have no impact on the person at all in a particular situation. So let me give you an example. There is a gene that is called the transforming growth factor beta gene – it doesn't matter what it's called – TGF beta. And it turns out that if you have a particular sequence upstream of the gene, you live your normal life, whether you have Type A or Type B. But if you get irradiated for cancer, and you have Type A, you have more toxicity than you have if you have type B. Is that normal or abnormal? Well for most people it doesn't matter unless you are being irradiated in a particular tissue for cancer. So it is not that it is irrelevant. It is not always relevant to everybody in a particular room. And that, I think, may just be a simple polymorphism, rather than normal versus abnormal.

I think that there is going to be a lot of discussion about this idea of calling things mutants and abnormals. In today's sequencing world this is going to have to change drastically. So I think you are exactly right.

Population Normal in Quasispecies (0)

Comment. It seems to me that the study of very simple organisms such as viruses may give us a perspective on what is normal. In the case of HIV, for example, on which I've spent many years working, the virus changes so much that in any given individual you actually have a swarm of viruses. It is called a quasispecies. There is no absolute normal genotype that defines the population of this quasi species. That actually gives advantage to the organism because it is then able to survive within the immune surveillance of the host. I think viewing populations of higher species that way can be useful.

Gayle. I think that is a really good point. I will even go a step farther than that and say that cancer is the same thing. It is just that cancers are cells that come from our selves. They too, however, are swarms. In some cancer cells we find as many as 120 different mutations. Why? So the tumor can survive and evade the immune system. It is exactly the same story. And I think that is a way of thinking about it. All of those are abnormal for the host, if you look at it in the right way.

The Larger System Picture (2)

Comment. I am going to connect to something that was raised earlier about normality. It seems you are claiming that just because something is good for humans does not mean it is good for all the created order that humans are a part of. For example gluttony for humans is at the expense of some other creature. Human beings now use up 30% of the productivity of the planet. With that critique how should we decide what is normal? A mutation in my body might be abnormal for me and my species, but it sure is advantageous to a disease-causing agent that that might be present. So if we look at what is good in the sense of a systems approach and how the integrity of the ecological system and the social systems of which we are a part, it cautions us from being too anthropocentric.

Gayle. Yes, I think that is absolutely true. A mutation that makes a virus unable to infect the person is great for the person but is horrible for the virus. And we need to look at things in a broader sense than we do. So you are right, I agree.

8. Religion and Science

Unanswerable Questions in Science (1)

Question: Could you comment further on this idea of what is answerable and what is not answerable? Are there some things that might be not answerable in biology but could be answered in another scientific discipline?

And are there some questions that are not answerable by science at all, by definition? Is there something about the way we define science that means certain questions cannot be answered by science?

Gayle. That's a good question. I think the hardest thing is about reconstruction of the past. Maybe physicists will develop a time machine and that will solve all the problems. I don't know if I believe that. But there are some physicists I know who do. And some engineers who do. But short of that I think that reconstruction of the past always comes with uncertainty. We can try to go do the genetic espionage, then look at where the bones are found and things like that. But that always comes with the fact that we might not understand context very well. So we find much more uncertainty with disciplines like archaeology and physical anthropology that have to go back and to track back things in time.

Now there are some things we can learn with more certainty than others. For instance, most studies seem to suggest that humans came out of Africa. *Homo sapiens* came out of Africa. There are some people that will argue about that model, but the genetics seems to point to that. And we can go back into gene sequences for people from all different cultures. For example we can go back and do genetic studies for early humans who lived in Kenya and that area and, based on that, we can sort of show that everything came out of Africa. So that is maybe a certainty.

Less certain would then be the track that they took when they came out of Africa. Did they go into Asia or did they go into Europe? What is the order in which they went into these places? And did they interbreed? Were there other *Homo* species in some of those locations that had come earlier, that they interbred with? And I think that those become harder to define because they involve a cultural type of question. At least from a biology perspective, I find those as questions that are going to be very, very difficult to discern the farther back we go in time.

If we ask questions such as what did the first cell look like, or what was the first form of life that occurred on earth the questions become harder and harder because there is even less record. And much more speculation goes into it. We can guess, and they are still educated guesses, but that's all.

Time in Theology and in Science (1)

Question. In this conversation there seems to be a concept or a topic underlying everything, but hasn't been explicitly mentioned, and that is time. I'm really interested to see what your reflections are on some of the similarities and differences between how scientists deal with time versus how theology might. Specifically, for instance, evolution has a temporal element. But it doesn't have the same meaning that it does in theology. Specifically Christianity sees time in a radically different way, and places the possibility of meaning on time. Time has a different weight there. How do you think the difference plays out? Is there the potential for a dialogue on the issue of time?

Gayle. From a Christian perspective there is a distinction in how time is viewed. In the one sense we view time as being almost sacred, something that we set aside, something that is valued, that we revere. And we mark the day with certain church services, with certain approaches. Time is considered to be so precious that how we spend our time is very important as well. I think that is true from a Christian perspective.

But there is also the Christian idea that, in a sense, we are in an eternal time. So Sunday is not the seventh day, it is the eighth day of the week. It is out of time. In my tradition, which is the Orthodox tradition, we do not say Christ was risen two thousand years ago. We greet each other with Christ is risen, in that eternal now that is. So I think that from the Christian perspective we see both of those viewpoints working their way into the system. When we are repeating a liturgy, we are repeating forever the eternal event that was initiated two thousand years ago.

So I think there is a sort of play on time that is different from what we find scientifically. There we are looking at time in that physical sense that is marked by the day, by the year, by real physical things that we can monitor.

Christians do monitor time in that same way, but probably see it slightly differently because it is set aside in a special way, in a theological way. The scientist is trying to look at time more from standpoint of the question, "How did things change? How did they progress?" This is almost in a physical sense, even though time isn't so physical.

One thing I will say from Bulgakov,[70] whom I mentioned last night, is that Bulgakov says that time is a human thing. We probably need time in order to survive. But, what is time to God? The things that happened today are a memory to God. And that becomes a different way of thinking about it. We can try to anthropomorphize God, and believe that the way we understand things temporally is the way in which things happen temporally in God's domain. So I don't think I have really answered your question, but I talked around it.

Question (continued). Actually that answer was really helpful. But to complete the answer what do you think the dangers are that might occur with theologians and scientists having slightly different conceptions of time when they are talking to one another? And at the same time, what are the possibilities? It seems like with these two dimensions we could come up with a better understanding through dialogue.

Gayle. The theological idea of time is actually a human thing. Fifty percent of scientists are non-believing. They are atheists. But they value time with their families, they value time in a different sense than just the physical time we talked about scientifically. So that sort of relationship is a human relationship. And I think that you can always appeal to people's humanity when you are dealing with those issues. This morning we were talking about time balance at breakfast. I mean balancing time is what every human being has to do. So when you relate at the human level to scientists, then you can sort of get to that same idea of theological time, because I think they are kind of the same, just understood slightly differently.

Religion and Scientific Observation (2)

Question. I have talked with various professors about how we relate science and religion, traditional religion. There were good biblical reasons to think the earth stood still. For instance Joshua commanded the sun to stand still. But science spoke loudly and the data were clear. So we had to rethink our theology. How large do you think the tipping points should be? How long should we hold to tradition? And then how loud does science have to speak

---

[70] Sergius Nikolaevich Bulgakov (1871 – 1944) was a Russian Orthodox Christian theologian, philosopher, and economist.

before we re-evaluate our theology?

Gayle. Well, evolution fits along that same story, right? I believe that we need always to be open.

Since every person in this room who prays is a theologian, we must all of us be open to new ideas and new thoughts. And when something in particular grates against what we are used to, I think it needs to be examined and looked at, and then answered.

Those quotes, such as when the sun stood still, requiring a geocentric component were found in the Old Testament. Again a lot of those were metaphoric. They weren't meant to be that precise. But for the understanding of the Bible at the time, that is how they took that. Now, I don't know that the understanding was bad for them, in that it mattered for their faith whether they believed that the sun stood still or not. But certainly it is bad when now evidence tells you one thing, and you believe the opposite. I think that is a harmful thing. So did it hurt people for a thousand years to believe that the sun moved around the earth? Did it hurt their faith, anybody's faith, for those thousand years? No. But when science shows something, and reveals something to us, then to deny it, I think, becomes harmful, because then we are denying a truth.

So the Catholic Church (and I believe they took a lot of grief over this) went through a lot of heart ache to be able to come to right conclusions about this. But they did come to the right conclusions.

And now look at the difficulty we are in over evolution, and probably will be for some time to come. And it was discovered in 1860s.[71] I mean, that is really a long time. But we are in the throes of this, and we are going to have to go through it. It may also be different for every one of those kinds of arguments.

Religion and Evolution (2)

Question. And so for you it is not so much a tipping point where enough evidence is amassed. The issue is how much theological harm will be done if we accept this new idea. I think that is what people are trying to balance.

---

[71] *On the Origin of Species* went on sale to booksellers on 22 November 1859. It was already oversubscribed.

Gayle. I know. But I believe that is actually a wrong way of thinking about it. If we know something and we deny it, then we are hurting humanity as a whole. So what we need to do is to figure out what those perceived issues are that hurt the church or the faith, and deal with those. For instance, I know the evolution story better because it is in modern times. People deny evolution because it teaches rabid materialism. So it denies the spiritual. It accepts the material. And, therefore, it is bad. People deny evolution because it puts us on par with the animals. And there are a thousand reasons why people who are religious, from a spiritual perspective, can argue from their own religious tradition that accepting evolution is wrong.

But I would argue the exact opposite, that if all the facts say that evolution is true, and the church denies those facts, then the church is hurting itself and becomes irrelevant to everything. The church needs to deal with what is the truth and why those problems are issues.

Does evolution really teach only materialism? Well, evolution was only meant to explain the material, so of course it does. It's not up to scientists to tell you where God goes in that story. It's up to theologians to do that. I tell you for a fact that I do not want any scientist telling me how God fits in the evolution story, because I don't know which God they picked to put in, if any. So we are better off dealing with this the way we are doing it, which is that the science deals with the science, and theology deals with the theology. Those of us who are in this room, who are having this dialogue about this, let us try our best to put them together, but let us do it truthfully.

Religion and Scientific Theory (2)

Comment. I have a comment on the question of the sun and the Church's position. Galileo was pretty certain about the Copernican model with the sun as central and the planets moving around the sun. But was there really any reason for the Church to change its concept of the universe at that point? There wasn't very much evidence. Once Newton had a mechanism for why then I think that was the ultimate Yes. If you have a mechanism we should believe you. There must to be some kind of tipping point. What do you mean by knowing?

Gayle. Knowing is that point when a model, that is a scientific model, becomes what we would call a Theory in science.

Let me distinguish. There is this capital "T" Theory thing, and the small "t" theory thing. An example of the small "t" theory thing is that I have a theory that my boss doesn't like me because he didn't tell me how good my data look. That is the small "t" theory thing that we talk about in ordinary conversation. But that is actually not how scientists use the word Theory. The word Theory in science is with a capital T, and it means there is a huge body of literature, a huge body of science, that all comes together and supports this one big Theory.

I have this diagram of a sheep leaping in the air, and saying, "Gravity, just a theory."

So when Galileo's ideas moved from the realm of being an hypothesis to being a Theory, which meant that there was a substantial body of evidence to support it, including Newton's Theory of gravity, then I think that the Church had to do something about it in a real sense.

You can have a zillion little ideas out there that come out, and nobody ever knows about them. But once they reach that status of being a Theory, then that is when it hits. And it is interesting that both of these issues, the Theory of evolution or the Theory of gravity, generated such a big hoopla within the religious communities.

Comment. Thank you very much. That is an excellent answer.

Influence of Science on Religion (2)

Comment. It seems to me that there is a utilitarian reason for the church to be on top of scientific Theories (capital "T"). Once the church has accepted a Theory a whole new realm of exploration of God is opened. And the church came to some new comprehension of God because of the acceptance of heliocentrism. Evolution is the Theory on which I have read the most. But then I began wondering, what about something like physics. I am not sure that quite fits in the same way because it is so incredibly difficult for lay people to understand, but maybe there is something in the future there, too.

Gayle. I have a friend who is an exobiologist who studies the potential for life on other planets. She is convinced that this is going to open a new dimension for our church communities as well. So I agree with you. It may be a very good thing that we open up some new dimensions. We can argue that these are also things that are revealed to us as humanity. And we need to look at them as revealed truths too.

Comment (Continued). John Polkinghorne has written some about physics, quantum mechanics and that sort of thing.

Gayle. Yes he has done a really good job with that. I am not a physicist, I have limited physics capabilities and I rely on Polkinghorne a lot for that stuff. He's very good.

Comment. I am one of the physicists here. Of course Polkinghorne is someone to look at, and I like to read Polkinghorne as well. But he once said something to the effect that we should not worry about quantum theory, because it's going to all sort of work its way out in the fact that we are looking at macroscopic systems. He may be right. But I wonder often about the brain, because physiologically that is the place where we are closest to a quantum system. There we remain remarkably more molecular and even electronic at the nerve transmission and interactive level. And there are also diffusion processes involved in neural transmission that make me wonder at points. So in answer to the idea of where is quantum theory possibly going to be important, as a physicist I would wonder about our understanding of the brain.

Comment. A year or two ago at the Grand Dialogue[72] in Grand Rapids one of the sessions was on quantum mechanics and the brain. A topic in that session was on a possible site, or sites, where our immaterial soul could actually influence things at the quantum mechanical level to cause brain interaction. One group had proposed two or three sites. So people are looking into that, and I thought that is really interesting.

Comment. I think that the notion that we don't really need to worry about quantum effects at the macroscopic scale is becoming harder and harder to defend. We have now shown quantum entangled macro states. So just the notion of sweeping quantum effects under the rug, because ithey are tiny, I

---

[72] The Grand Dialogue is an annual conference on religion and scince held at Grand Rapids, MI.

think, is getting harder to defend.

Gayle. Well, the one thing that goes along with quantum thinking anyway, is that at the very small scale things actually have a different chemistry. And they behave differently. When you start to look at nanomaterials, for instance, we find that they have a very different chemistry than materials at the micro scale. And that may actually play into this as well with these things getting very small, it might be because you are looking at a kind of different chemistry there, too.

Interwoven Biology and Theology (3)

Question. I appreciate the way in which you have woven the themes of relationships through biology and theology together.

Can you clarify what you meant when you talked about hypostasis in personhood in terms of biology? I think you used the word otherworldly. The dynamics seems to be more about our biology and how it has adapted us and devoid of the theme of relationship that an ecological paradigm would help us understand.

I am wondering what we are skirting around here with suffering and pain, and whether it will always be present in nature. Does this result from the biological fact that we are inextricably connected to all other manner of life? Even if we make the right choices and do not try to dominate the habitat, biology is still going to impose suffering upon us. In that sense it seems that the biology has a lot to teach us about otherworldliness.

Gayle. One of the hard things is that I believe that these two are interfused together. I make a distinction because it is easier to understand.

We may consider the first part to be a biological relationship. But you know, a relationship that creates a human being is much more than biological, there is a spiritual dimension to it. And in any situation there is not just the relationship between the two people, but there is the relationship with God. So there is an otherworldliness component to it, too.

I do not think that the biology and the otherworldliness are fully separated. I think they are intermingled. But unless I tease them apart, I can't explain how they work. Now if you throw in a relationship with the environment and the world, then there is both a biological dimension and an otherworldliness dimension to all of it. I really believe that in all relationships of two human beings, five human beings, one-hundred human beings, there is always an otherworldly component to it.

9. Religion

Insight from the Orthodox Tradition (1)

Question. You have given us some quotes from people in the Orthodox tradition and you yourself represent that. Could you give us an idea of what the Orthodox position might contribute to both the Protestant and the Catholic traditions in this dialogue between religion and science, and what kinds of things may we be looking for in the next lectures?

Gayle. I am not sure that there is so much distinction between the Orthodox, and the Catholic and the Protestant view on many of these things, because we shared a history and a basis of 4000 years.[73] And I think we can go back, all of us, to many of the same features that we would think are important and see common themes and common similarities. So when I talk about [Sergei] Bulgakov as an Orthodox theologian, I think of his theology as a broad theology that doesn't just apply to Orthodox, it applies in a broad sense. And there are many Catholic scholars and Protestant scholars who are discovering him, and quoting him as being an important teacher for our time. I don't think that it is unique. And I don't think that what I am saying is uniquely Orthodox in that sense. Probably you could say it's Christian. I'm not sure I can speak from a Jewish perspective or anything else, but I do think it is sort of more broadly Christian.

That said, let me talk specifically about how Orthodox can contribute to the discussion that is going on. You know, Orthodox have a different history. We did not go through the Enlightenment in the same way as Western Europe and much of the Orthodox Church was held captive by communism or by the Ottoman Empire. For several centuries Orthodox reflections were not part of our broad society.

And yet I would say that in the last fifty or one-hundred years there has been a reawakening of Orthodox thinking and scholarship. And with that

[73] This includes Hebrew history.

comes a sort of openness. The Orthodox Church doesn't introduce as many dogmas as everybody else. There tends to be a breadth in what the Orthodox Church understands. There is a great deal of tolerance for thinking out of the box, and a great deal of tolerance for different ideas, because creativity is seen to come from different ideas. Although some people thought him a heretic, Bulgakov himself was never excommunicated or considered to be a heretic because that's just not so common among the Orthodox. So I think there is sort of an openness that the Orthodox might be able to bring to the table that might be helpful. At least I hope so.

Genesis and History (1)

Question. Yesterday you were talking about Bulgakov when you said that the creation story in Genesis is considered as a meta-history. It is something yet to come. Wouldn't that negate the validity of the entire Bible? Can you elaborate on that?

Gayle. I'm not a biblical scholar, but all my biblical courses have taught me several things.

First of all I believe that most people, including Jewish scholars, would argue that the first actual historical event in Genesis is Abraham. And anything before that is very open to interpretation. So it was written with a different texture. It was written with a different perspective. And there are multiple stories that often conflict with each other. For instance, there is the Genesis 1 story, which tells one story of the origin. Then there is the Genesis 2 story that tells of a different origin. And they are actually in conflict with each other. How do we resolve those?

The same thing is true with the flood story of Noah, where again there are two stories of the flood. Which one is the right one? There is a mixture of different stories because they are not historical. They are meant more to tell us something deeper about humanity; a meta-story about deep understandings rather than anything else.

I will also say that there are other inconsistencies with Genesis and other portions of the Bible. There is a creation story in Job, there is a creation story in Psalms. So you can find multiple different creation stories. Which one do you accept?

A better understanding of the creation story is that they were never actually trying to write a history. They were trying to tell us something about humanity that we need to understand. And what are those things that we need to understand? We need to understand that creation was made good. When humanity came along, creation was made very good. When creation took place, humanity was meant to be in relationship with God and in relationship with other persons and that humanity has a relationship with creation. Then Adam named the animals, and there is a relationship in naming the animals that is very important. So if we treat it as history, we almost lose the meaning of the story of who we are as humans, and some deep sense of understanding. So I think there is a better approach to it.

I also think that if you could read the Hebrew you would know that Adam is not really one person. Adam means from the ground, from the soil. And Eve means mother of all. And if you see those not so much as first names but as meaning something broad, I think it gives a much deeper understanding.

So I would tend to agree with biblical scholars that perhaps Abraham is the moment when we can start thinking about history. But even those stories beyond Abraham are not totally historical. There are parts of those that are meant to tell us things about each of those people they talk about.

For instance there is a story of Jacob, who has two wives, the daughters of Laban his relative. [Genesis 29-31] Jacob has worked seven years for each wife and then wants to return to the country of his people. But Laban says, "No," and asks Jacob to name the wages that will make him stay. Jacob asks Laban to let him pass through the flocks and select the black sheep and the speckled and spotted sheep and goats as his wages.

Then Jacob spends time trying to build up a group of sheep and goats that he can take with him. The text says the sheep and goats breed when they are taken to water. So Jacob prepares poplar and almond sticks by cutting streaks in them to expose the white. And he puts out sticks so that when the sheep and goats breed they see the stripes and the flocks would bring forth striped, speckled and spotted young. He could then take all these young sheep and goats with him.

Now we know that doesn't happen. I don't think that this intends to tell

us that the laws of nature were different then than they are now. I think that
that story is meant to tell us that Jacob was a smart man, and that he could
trick his father-in-law into giving him what was right, and was lawfully his.
He could outwit Laban.

So we have to take this story for what it is intended to tell us, not as a
history. Reading of the Bible, I think, has to be cautiously done. The Bible is
not just something that we read and try to take literally.

Grace in the Orthodox Church (2)

Question. Last night you were exploring normal, deviation and variety. For
philosophers those concepts demand some sort of analysis. When genetic
errors occur the results may be productive, or they may also be dangerous.
But we never use a neutral word to describe this. Similarly scientists can
handle chance as something that is not necessarily negative. But in common
usage chance is secondary to planned. Is there any concept in theology that
is similar to chance? In the Orthodox tradition the notion of grace has to be
a bit different than in the West. How do you integrate, or do you integrate,
those notions into your own person?

Gayle. I need to think about that one a little bit.

The idea of grace we do understand slightly differently in the Orthodox
Church than everybody else does. But it is only a slight difference. It is not
significant. I think we understand it. It's available to everybody. It is something
that comes sort of naturally under the appropriate circumstances. So grace
is understood maybe in a broader sense for Orthodox. And it's even possible
for people that are outside of the tradition to experience grace. So it is a very
broad sort of term for us.

I had this idea in the discussion with the students this afternoon. I think
that life is about a journey. And I hope that journey is towards some sort
of truth or some sort of rightness. A lot of times things come in your path
that you don't expect but that place you better on that path, on that journey.
And that might feel like chance that tells you something, that influences you
and puts you more on the straight path instead of on a divergent path, even
though it could come from a person that you don't like.

Now I told the old joke that we tell among at least many people I know.

We say that if God could talk out of Balaam's ass, he could certainly talk out of anybody you know. And if that is true then we have to be open to hear things from anybody. And we need to be open at the right moment to hear those things. That could actually be very much like chance, I think. Because you're tired you may be open or closed depending on the circumstance. And that may relate to grace then, because to some extent that grace is that openness to hearing what you are going to hear. So I think it is really an interesting thought.

Sin and Inheritance (2)

Comment. Earlier today in your lecture you asked whether sin is genetic. It seems to me that if it is genetic it disappears from our consciousness. Then we could argue that there would be no such thing as sin.

Gayle. Yes, thank you for that. That came up in the student session today, too. So let me clarify and be sure that I am saying at least my own thoughts correctly.

If there is anything, there might be a genetic tendency toward sin. But I don't believe that there is a genetic program that makes us sin. So let's use the example of alcoholism, because it's an easy one where we know there is a genetic tendency, and it is something that is inherited, that is the tendency is inherited. It's also something that is modulated by the person's behavior.

All of us have been dealt difficult deals, some of them are in our family members, some of them are in our genes, some of them are in our environment, and some of them are in our own abilities and lack of abilities. But if the goal is to sort of walk that straight and narrow path of not sinning then we have to struggle to reach that goal. In some cases maybe we are struggling against our own genetics. And in some cases we are struggling against our upbringing, our families, or our workplace. But it is a struggle. And I think that we are called to make that struggle, even if it is against our own genetics.

So I don't believe that we inherit sin. But we all inherit somehow the ability to sin, and we must struggle against that.

The original word for sin is interesting. It comes from a Greek word *amartia* (or *hamartia*). This word was used in reference to an archer. When the archer hit the mark the term used was *martia*. And when the archer missed the mark the term used was *amartia*. And that was the word that eventually became sin in the Latin connotation, which was also a missing of the mark.

It didn't have the same connotation, I think, that it has in our society. It means that you didn't hit the bull's-eye. But, you know what? You keep trying to go down that straight path, you keep trying to hit that bull's-eye, and sometimes you will miss, but then you just get up and you do it again until you hit it. That thinking makes some sense to me.

Understanding and Temptation (2)

Question. There is an example that I give to my students. We understand that our cravings for sugar are partly, not completely, biological in nature, due to adaptations in some prehistoric time when sugar was rare. Then when I see a candy bar or a soda, I can say, "Hah! No way! I'm not falling prey to that. That was for my ancestors to be adaptive to a different environment. It's not helping me." So at some level as I understand my predispositions, which we may call sin in some religious communities, I get more freedom of choice, because then I have the power to act. That may be seen as ironic.

Gayle Yes, I really like that idea. I think that that is really exactly correct. The more awareness we have of where things come from and what drives our inappropriate or unhealthy desires, we can actually try to root it out.

That assumes that you always want to be on the right track. And there are some people who will say, "I don't really care, I'm just going to do what I want to do because that is not important in my life."

But then again at least people have that choice. And maybe through an understanding of it, we can at least help put some people to get on the right track. So I think it is really a good idea. I like that thought.

Sin and Survival (2)

Question. About five years ago I read a very clever essay showing the incompatibility of theology and science. The author analyzed the seven capital sins showing that, from the point of view of survival, these are not sins at all. I was struck by the discussion of gluttony. The author claimed that gluttony is not just good for the individual, but for the species. To hurry to the kill or crowd something else out of the kill is going to increase the survival ability. But theology says that is a bad habit to get into. He went on through with lust and pride and the others as well. It was a clever piece.

Gayle. From experience, I'm not sure I would agree that gluttony is good for you healthwise. I don't think it is good for the species either. And I could make arguments against many of the other things.

There are things that I find interesting in those sorts of arguments. There was a good discussion on altruism and genetics, as presented by Richard Dawkins, in the discussion this morning. There have also been new studies that show altruism also counts when you are picking your spouse. More people would like to pick an altruistic spouse then a non-altruistic spouse. You can think about why that might be true. There may then really be a selective advantage for these positive attributes, these things that we would, at least from a spiritual dimension, consider positive attributes in humanity. It may not be all about selection for what is genetically best or what seems like it is best on the surface, because we are very complicated. My dog might only care about the next meal. But that is not always how people think about things. So, this is interesting.

Free Will Action Potential (2)

Question. In one of my classes we discussed the point that maybe we don't so much have free will as free won't. In some studies it apprears that we have an action potential set up in the brain, which disappears before the person consciously makes a decision, like to pick up something. What it means to be free is very complicated.

Gayle. It's an interesting thought.

I tend to believe that it is not just about always rejecting bad, it's also about sometimes choosing good. So I would say it it's not just about won't it's about will, too. But those two go hand-in-hand and it's hard to divorce them.

10. Suffering
Suffering and Religion (3)

Question. You correctly pointed out the difference between pain and suffering, and the reflective nature of suffering. Because of the reflective nature of suffering I wonder if we may claim that religion eliminates suffering rather than accepting suffering as inevitable.

Pain is inevitable. We are biological beings. But religion gives us an opportunity to see pain in other ways. You spoke of suffering as a perception of pain and the desire to stop it, while religion moves us beyond that desire to stop pain or to see pain in a more positive way. We may then be able to move beyond suffering.

I do not think we will ever be able to move to a point of equanimity to pain, blissfully ignoring it. But I wonder if the issue of suffering and religion is more complicated.

Gayle. I agree with you and I disagree with you. So let me do my do my best to explain.

I think that the path toward a resolution of suffering, I don't want to say elimination, does come through religion. But when I meet people that I consider to be holy, who have written about suffering, I find that the suffering takes on a different nature. They no longer suffer for themselves, they suffer for others. They feel such compassion for others that they now feel their suffering and take it upon themselves. And they pray for that suffering to be handled properly. So every time somebody they know is suffering and not handling it, they suffer too.

So I think that that suffering can be very, very broad or very personal. These people feel it personally in that same sense. And I think, to some extent, that we are called to have that compassion too. So I wouldn't say that religion removes it, but it certainly helps us handle it, or it makes us put it in a different context. But I think you cannot be a person who does not suffer in any religious context. If you are, you are probably not a real person.

If you love others, you suffer when they die. If you love others, you suffer when they are sick. You suffer with them. And that suffering never goes away, even though you pray about it and everything else, there is still a part of you inside that hurts. And if you didn't hurt you wouldn't be human.

Suffering and Free Will (3)

Question. You said that suffering is a requirement of free will. I can understand how it would be a result of free will, but I was wondering if you could expand on what you mean that it is a requirement.

Gayle. I think suffering is a requirement of humanity, because free will gives everybody a choice to do right or wrong. Some people are going to choose to do wrong no matter what. It's going to happen. And when people choose to do wrong the result is suffering.

Consider that somebody steals your stereo. You are going to suffer for that. It might be a small suffering, but you are going to suffer for that. If somebody kills one million people humanity is going to suffer.

Everybody can choose right or wrong. We all miss the mark sometimes.

Suffering and Free Will (3)

Question. I was confused on a point you made about free will and suffering. If you were to assume that we lived in a world with no free will – which I know we don't – and everything was considered to be good, there would be no bad. But natural disasters would still make people suffer. That conflicts with the point that free will causes suffering. Could you speak to that?

Gayle. Suffering is a broad word. And there is a sense in which we choose to suffer.

What I mean is, if there is an earthquake in Asia and you don't feel anything at all, or if your best friend dies and you don't feel anything at all, that is your free will. You can choose to not feel anything. You choose not to suffer. But what will happen is you will feel it somehow. It is going to come out of you in different ways. We all know of cases in which someone whose parent, or sister or brother died, just decided, "I'm going to go on with life, and I'm going to ignore this." They choose not to suffer for it. So then what happens? Because they are human they will pay a price for it later.

I do think that to some extent suffering is a choice. I think there is a part of suffering which people can choose to turn off, and there are ways in which people do that in our culture. They drink lots of alcohol, and sometimes even that doesn't turn it off, and then they do drugs. They have escapism.

They have things that that they do to keep them preoccupied. They do video games for twelve hours a day and never let anything in. So they don't think about the brother that died. He's gone. But that choice to suffer, I think, is very, very important.

I don't want to say that all suffering is a choice. But even many people that have cancer choose to deny that it is there. They believe that they are never going to die and that technology is going to save them. So they choose not to suffer. There is a component of choice to it.

Suffering and Heaven (3)

Question. Yesterday, in the student discussion, we talked about heaven, where I assume there would still be free will, but there would be no suffering.

Gayle. And I told you then and I'll say it again. I have no idea what heaven looks like. So I am not going to conjecture what we might look like in heaven. I just believe it is there.

Suffering and Contentment (3)

Question. In Philippians Paul claims he has learned to be content in all things. Would you define contentedness and lack of suffering differently, or has Paul managed to overcome suffering through the power of God? Do we only have to suffer until God takes it away?

Gayle. Good question.

I think that contentment is contentment with suffering as well. Elsewhere Paul talks about his own sufferings and his problems with his back and other things. It is not that they never bother him. But you just become content with it. This is what God dealt me today, okay. And you go on. It doesn't mean you don't feel it, it doesn't mean that you don't feel any pain, but it expresses itself in a contentment that God has given you this, and you will accept it as his will.

Joy in Suffering (3)

Question. To me being content sounds very much like being happy which is contrary to suffering.

I don't think you'll find the word happy in any of Paul's writing, at least not as translated from the original Greek. Happiness means something very different, and we have to be very cautious with that word. What happiness meant say in the US during the 1700s when the Constitution was written, is not the same as what it means today. Happiness meant that you had freedom to be a good person. That's contentment, maybe. But that's not the happiness that you talk about today as happy, happy, joy, joy.

Gayle. Right. I was not referring to happiness as happy, happy, joy, joy.

And let me just say that there are people that do find joy in their suffering. I don't think I can do this. Certainly I have never reached that point. But there are people who are happy. They are joyful that they are suffering because they will grow from it, because they will gain something from it. Paul even says at one point, "I'm thankful that God gave me this burden. It makes me better." So there are people that can feel happiness and joy in suffering. But it is again that acceptance of the suffering that is first so important.

Mentally Overcoming Suffering (3)

Question. In our student session we spoke of the power of the brain to just think away suffering. Over the last few years I been personally experimenting with the concept of reimagining pain as a notification that my body is giving me that I can choose to ignore if I so desire. It's surprising if you choose to think of something a certain way, how it can radically change how you feel about it. Does this apparent power of the brain to affect how the body feels have a biological basis? Is it something that God allows to happen? Or is there a mix of the two?

Gayle. I have oncologist friends who see patients come in with giant tumors protruding from their bodies, and they always say, "Denial ain't just the river in Egypt."

People go denying these problems for a very, very long time. And their minds, their psyches, somehow have convinced them that this protuberance is something else. It's not important. And many psychological studies show that that kind of mind alteration, that denial, can be very helpful and very useful.

In fact in early development this is a mechanism for coping with problems in a family. When you are six, seven, eight years old, ten years old, twelve years old, those denial mechanisms help people to survive. So they are not always bad. It is not always a bad thing to deny it. But there is a point at which you need to overcome that.

That might not be exactly the same mechanism that you are talking about. But I believe it is related, because both involve mental approaches to try to suppress painful events. And whether those painful things are physical or whether they are emotional-psychological, certainly people use that to help them through difficult times. It's just that if you keep denying it, we know it's going to come back to hurt you.

Mind over Discomfort (3)

Question. Denial is not at all what I was talking about. As an example, I like to end my showers with freezing cold water. At first it was really, really difficult. I'm not denying that I am being covered in freezing cold water. But I adjust my mind to the point at which I view the event differently. I think it is possible to do this with emotional events as well. You're not denying them. You are just coping with it differently. I do not believe that is an unhealthy method.

Gayle. I think the distinction is that I am not sure I would call your cold water experience the same thing as suffering through a death, or suffering through an illness that is life-threatening. And so I think it is all about terms.

In Korea they actually send their troops out into freezing, cold weather with no clothes on, so that they become better acclimated and will be able to deal with environmental circumstances. That is known to be a way in which we help people through changing their minds and adjusting their bodies to cope with things. I don't think that is a wrong thing. I just think that even though denial of severe problems is healthy, or at least is necessary when you are young, there comes a point in time when you can't go on denying. It has to be a severe thing, however. It's not just these physical discomforts.

Buddhist Tradition of Accepting (3)

Comment. The Buddhist tradition treats this idea of overcoming initial pain or suffering leading to a sense of purity of mind. Through the acceptance of pain it can be transformed into compassion as you were mentioning. I have experienced this and seen it happen with my friends. There is an ignorance which is unhealthy because you are not addressing the problem, and then there is an acceptance. The book *Tuesdays with Morrie*[74] contains interviews with a man who says that he accepts pain, he experiences it, and then he lets it pass on. I think that is one thing that we as humans have to learn to do with death as well. We should, accept it for what it is, and then let it pass on.

As to free will causing suffering we need to remember the first thing that makes us a person. As you described today, we are in communion with other persons, and even in communion with other agencies, such as the natural world. We all have needs, wants, and desires, which will always conflict with someone else's. Even in an intimate relationship there is always one who is giving more or taking more at any instant. That goes along with natural disasters. The earth plates need to move to do what they need to do, and that is going to cause eruptions, and that is going to cause havoc on human societies and communities.

Ayn Rand[75] thought that a perfect world would result if each individual sought for the best for themselves.

If you are thinking about heaven as a place that does not have biological needs, then you may be able to have free will and also be able to have this idea of no suffering. Because you won't have conflicting needs, if everything is provided. So you may lose free will. But you will be at perfect peace and happy in that sense.

Gayle. Thank you very much. I don't have much to add to it, you did a really good job of expressing it. So thank you.

Suffering Shared in Speech (3)

Question. The biblical metaphor in both stories of creation in Genesis is God speaks, or God breathes. It's the same emotion, the same action. And

---

[74] Mitch Albom, *Tuesdays with Morrie* (New York: Doubleday, 1997).
[75] Ayn Rand (1905-1982) was Russian-American author, playwrite and philosopher.

people doing pastoral ministry in hospitals tell me the same thing. Part of the power of speech exercised by someone who is sick, someone who is suffering, is letting that suffering be shared by other people. That is a gift that the suffering person gives to the caregiver. Patients are giving you something to share with them, creating a community there. This is another dimension of suffering.

Gayle. Very nice. Very beautiful.

Suffering from Evolution (3)

Question. Is there anything about suffering and response to pain that can be learned from the idea that we are the product of evolution and the process of evolution frequently causes suffering and pain at almost all levels of at least animal life?

Gayle. Yes, it's a good thought. We are certainly the product of our evolution and it's a painful process.

We stand upright. But our backs were never meant to be for creatures that stand upright, at least in their original design. And so we almost all have lumbar pain as we get older. And our joints were never meant to be able to do a lot of the things that we do with them. Then we have arthritic pain. So that is a product actually of our evolution. I believe that it may be inherent in the process. There is a science joke that if I had to design a back, I wouldn't design it the way we have it.

So I think you are right that suffering may be a natural product of our evolution. There will be some forms of suffering that are required just because we are evolved creatures. We know certain dog strains have certain problems in the way that their backs are designed or their limbs are designed so that they are always displaced. And it has to do again with the fact that they evolved originally from wolves that were able to run long distances, and now they are in a more confined environment and they can't run so well.

So I think that is true. Our evolution itself may create some of our suffering.

And cancer may be a product of evolution too, to some extent.

Honestly. We talk about that often. In fact there is a guy, Leonard Hummel[76] in Gettysburg, PA, who is writing a book on cancer and evolution. I am involved in his book project. There are two aspects to his thinking on that. First of all cancer may be inevitable in human evolution because our cells are sort of pushed to divide a lot. And then over-pushing them happens inevitably. But then once the cancer is inside you, it also evolves. So there may be many aspects through our diseases that we get that are part of our evolution. It's a really nice idea.

Suffering and Christ's Teaching (3)

Comment. My understanding of the work of Christ is that a primary reason that Christ came was to teach us that suffering and death are okay. Christ suffered intensely, and still had a very close relationship with God. As humans we tend to think that if we are suffering that we are being separated from the divine, and that there is a fault accountable for that suffering. Our need to take control is the original sin. Christ teaches us that even in our suffering we can maintain a close and vital relationship with God. And that is central to our salvation from ourselves, which is what we all need.

Gayle. I agree with you. I agree with everything you said. Thank you.

Suiffering and God's Emotions (3)

Comment. If suffering requires free will, and suffering requires some emotional hurt, I think the Bible suggests that God exhibits emotions, he changes his mind.

Gayle. Certainly Christ weeps.

God Suffers (3)

Editor's Comment: The exchange which follows is short, but difficult. The issue is not easy and requires that we consider God to have human emotions. I have left the wording almost untouched. Peggy Schott, a chemist from Northwestern University, was the Homilist.

---

[76] Leonard Hummel is professor of pastoral theology and pastoral care at the Lutheran Theological Seminary in Gettysburg, PA.

Comment. Christ weeps, certainly. He was also human and God, and so I don't know how you want to put that. But I wonder if God suffers. I don't think God feels pain. This is hard to talk about.

Gayle. Did Peggy talk about that this morning in her homily? Why don't you repeat that thought, Peggy?

Peggy. Yes, I did talk about this as portrayed by the prophet Hosea. And it got me to thinking about whether God suffers. I believe there is a possibility that God suffers as God watches. It's hard not to use anthropomorphic language. But as God is with us, as God watches our fumbling's around, our choice making. Because I believe we do have free will to do good or bad, I think it is a helpful idea that God may suffer, because I care about that. How do I feel about God's suffering? The Old Testament prophets had that notion. And apparently God suffered greatly. I'll leave it at that.

Gayle. I'll comment, too, although, unfortunately, probably no one else in the room, or very few, will agree with me on this. But the way I think my tradition would understand God's suffering is in the fact that Christ suffered. We know Christ suffered. He suffered on the cross. And in humility, there is a divine humility; he emptied himself in order to allow his own death. And he is a person in the holy Trinity, who are in a communion of three persons in one. Therefore God the father, in his compassion, suffered with his son. So that is something that God, in his compassion, suffers for each one of us. That would be my answer, which agrees with Peggy.

Comment. We discussed God and free will in our student session, and that God sees all at once. That goes hand-in-hand with God's feeling all emotions at once. If God knows everything that is going to happen from the beginning of time, then he would also feel those emotions at the same time.

Gayle. I'm afraid to talk too much about God's emotions because I think it is anthropomorphizing a bit. But I do think that somehow God knows everything we experience, and somehow in his compassion he feels everything we experience. But I would be afraid to say much more than that. You know, it is still mystery.

A meaning in suffering (3)

Question. In Isaiah 53:11 we find, "He will see the travail of his soul, and be satisfied." And I noted your comment about purpose. I wonder if what makes something meaningful and what helps us to accept it is that we see the purpose of it in the end, and why we have to go through this. Do you have any thoughts about that?

Editor's Comment: The verse to which the question refers [Isaiah 53:11] is part of a poem identified as the *Fourth song of the servant of YHWH* [Jerusalem Bible]. The song begins with Isaiah 52:13 and ends with 53:11-12. In Isaiah 52:12 we have the beginning of the song as, "*See, my servant will prosper, he shall be lifted up, exalted, rise to great heights.*" Then Isaiah 53:10, 11 are

> *YHWH has been pleased to crush him with suffering.*
> *If he offers his life in atonement,*
> *he shall see his heirs, he shall have a long life*
> *and through him what YHWH wishes will be done.*

> *His soul's anguish over*
> *he shall see the light and be content.*
> *By his sufferings shall my servant justify many,*
> *taking their faults on himself.*
> *[The Jerusalem Bible]*

The words "*he shall see the light and be content,*" which in the RSV are, "*he shall see the fault of the travail of his soul and be satisfied,*" are those to which the question refers.

Gayle. I think that is the hard part too though. As human beings we always want to know why. This is like a crazy thing, but every person I know that gets cancer – I work with them a lot – wants to know, "Why did I get my cancer?" They look for physical causes. Did I eat the wrong foods? What did I do? And then they try to look for spiritual causes, like why, why did this happen to me? It's that why-me syndrome. And I do think there is always a purpose. But I think the way we discover that purpose is at the end, when we have worked through everything. And even then it still may remain mysterious to us. We may never know it until we are in heaven one day and all is revealed. But I don't think everybody walks away knowing the purpose for their suffering. Now maybe not everybody works through it right. I don't know. I just don't know. But I think it is a good thought that is worth thinking about.

Trust and Speaking (3)

Comment. You mentioned free will and the power of speech, although I am not sure you used the word power. One of the paradoxes of speech is that when we have an idea we give it up in speaking about it. It is released into the universe of other creative acts. But holding it in is understood in mysticism as the source of severe pain, the atrophying of who you are as a person.

Gayle. Let me comment on that.

When you talk to somebody there is a trust in the relationship, because they can do whatever they want with your idea. So being among scientists it is very common that you don't present your unpublished data at a conference. Now I'm an idiot. I do that. But many people do not do that because somebody might steal it and walk away. This is a sad reality today, but at many conferences for science, in the front row, you will see a bunch of people sitting there taking pictures of every slide that goes up. And we have to actually stop that at conferences so that people can feel some freedom to present. So there is in the word and in the presentation a given trust.

11. Thought
Origin of Ideas (2)

Question. There are no answers to the questions of what creativity is or what the source of ideas is. But you contrasted creativity to making a hypothesis and doing the experiment. We come from a lot of different backgrounds and have experienced creativity in a lot of different ways. Would you care to reflect on that?

Gayle. People often draw pictures of a scientist making discoveries. And they draw these eureka moments, where "then a miracle occurred" and you have some idea in your head.

That kind of eureka moment is an example of that creativity. You are nowhere. You don't have any idea at all. And then somehow in the craziest situation, in the weirdest moment, you now have an idea of how things work or how things fit together. And I think that is one way in which creativity works. But I also think there is a lot of creativity that comes from discussion. I'll talk about this tomorrow a little bit.

One of the reasons I try to have my students participate in discussions about their data is so that, as they listen to people talk, and as they themselves are forming their ideas to talk, they get new ideas that they didn't have before. So it's sort of a deliberate action of trying to think about something and bring it out in your words, and embody it in your words, that I think leads to creativity as well. And that is why meetings like this are so important. That's why scientific meetings are important. Because there are often many, many new ideas that come from our interacting with each other, not just from that eureka moment when somebody has this brilliant idea, or when they wake up in the middle of night with something new to think about.

I think that there are interaction issues that can also be associated with creativity. And that is why I think it is really critical to try to develop spaces where particularly students feel they can talk freely, because constraints on communication and being able to talk about things often hurt that creativity.

Thinking without Language (3)

Question. A colleague of mine here and I are artists. He and I both realize, and a number of people do not, that you can think without language. If you have done anything in art you realize that we do a lot of thinking without language. Do you want to comment on thought without language?

Gayle. That's a really good point. Long before we thought in language we thought in drawings. That goes back to ancient times. And certainly my students think with words and drawings. We actually draw pictures of how we envision things happening. So thank you so much, that's a good addition. I hadn't thought of saying that. But that is exactly right. I am really happy to hear you say it.

Thinking without Language (3)

Question. I don't know really anything about the development of written language. But if you look back at early Chinese characters, you find they are representational. For example the word for horse is a drawing of a stick-like horse figure. So the correlation has to be there. Surely it was there before we invented all these subtleties and extractions that worked for written language. However, I claim we need language to help refine and think about things that we couldn't think about otherwise.

Gayle. That brings up something that I probably should've said but I didn't.

No matter what, language falls short. When we are in that moment of silence with God, we are beyond language. Language falls short. So I don't want to lift up language as being something absolutely wonderful, and claim that it solves everything. I think language itself has problems.

We miscommunicate with each other often, particularly in this email age. For example somebody sends an email and says, "Oh, I'm furious." And somebody else says, "Why? And I was so kind in that email!" So clearly language can be harmful.

We still think in words. But we also think in thoughts that can be drawn. You know, a picture is worth 1000 words, as they say. And it's really true.

Index

D

E

F

G

M

malaria 64
martia 98
Meditation 41
mental disorders 43
Minnesota twin study 28
mitochondria 15

N

nanotechnology 30
natural law 74, 76, 81
Neanderthal 44
Neanderthal genes 68
Neanderthals 15
normal 83
normalcy 20
nuclear power 71
nuclear reactors 71

O

original sin 107
Orthodox tradition 93

P

pain 100
Peacocke, Arthur 63
Peirce, Charles Sanders 61
Philippians 102
philosophy 75
Planck Time 78
Polkinghorne, John 91
prosopon 35

Q

quasispecies 83

R

Rand, Ayn 105
RNA 74
Roman law 77

Made in the USA
Monee, IL
07 July 2026